CW01431121

Real Stories of Animal Communication No.8

by

'The Animal Psychic'

Jackie Weaver

Other books by the author:
Animal Insight
Animal Talking Tales
Celebrity Pet Talking
The Voice of Spirit Animals
Animal Communication from Heaven and Earth
For the Love of Pets
Real Animal Communications Stories No.7
Pet Grief – How to Cope Before and After

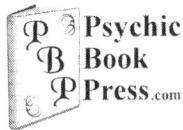

Psychic
Book
Press.com

ISBN 978- 1675636015

15th December 2019

I express huge gratitude to all
my friends for their continued
support, and help.
Thank you to all my wonderful
clients, and especially to those
who have contributed to this book.
Thanks to you, and your wonderful
animals, we can share more
real stories from my
world of animal communication.

Darling Sally2005- 2018

This is the last picture taken of Sally, the collie that really helped changed my life. I love the look on her face, which to me, was like she was saying, 'I know everything – I am a wise old soul' And she is... She told me I could communicate with the animals, and has helped me from day one, way back in 2007. She guides me, and has helped me to teach so many people. Even when she was ill in her final year, when I decided that a pupil should maybe chat to my cat instead, she took over anyway, giving me the unforgettable words...

'I am the teacher, and nothing will stop me doing that!'

Thank you Sally for being my inspiration, helper and most of all, for all the love you have shown me, Bob (my ex-husband – her 'dad') and other people.

Introduction

Welcome to my eighth animal communication book. I am blessed to know that many people buy these and know about me, my work and a bit of my life story too. So, in case you are new to my books, I will give you a brief outline...

I have now been involved in this wonderful world of communicating with animals, via their mind since 2007. I, the same as many people, never thought that this would be possible and quietly laughed to myself, thinking, 'As if!' Who would think that the writer of Dr Doolittle was far nearer the truth than they ever imagined and I would be working doing exactly that – talking to the animals.

My back-story is that I have survived what should have been terminal cancer in 2005 (stage 4 Lymphoma) and it truly changed my life, forever. I am not one of the type of psychics (which incidentally, psychic does not mean 'predicting the future' etc. but being able to tune to a wavelength to get information from a mind, person or animal) who wears floaty dresses and pretty flowery things in my hair. I do however wear smart dresses /jackets etc. when doing television work as hope to appeal to the broader audience and they realise that this is genuine and serious.

People describe me as very down-to-earth as I speak the truth and like to have fun. Although I take my work very seriously ethically, emotionally and responsibility wise, I spend much of my time laughing.

Animals have a sense of humour (well most) and I love to share their sense of fun with their owners. Many animals have problems / misunderstandings (like children and adults do) so I do my best to find out why, and try to help solve things. Another facet of my work is connecting to spirit animals for their owners. This is such a huge responsibility, as I know that people book me because they want to hear from their animal once again. Apart from missing their pets, and feeling totally heart-broken, they often carry unnecessary guilt about putting their beloved pets to sleep. They have to make that awful decision, which I know is out of love. I am the last person an owner would want to talk to, if it was not.

Talking about unnecessary guilt – although I say I have done eight books, it is actually nine as last year (2018) I brought out a different style of book. It is a self-help type to guide people with their pet grief, hence the title *Pet Grief – How to Cope Before and After*.

It has helped so many people in many different ways as can be seen on the Amazon reviews. It is full of techniques and things to help you understand your mind. I explain how we can do things to help ourselves through this grieving period and come out the other side, so once again we are able to think and smile about our spirit animal, without hurt and tears.

That is enough about me now, so on to this book. It is filled (as they all are) with totally genuine stories of people and their pets and the animal communication I did for them. I finish with a note from a lovely client couple, Kathy and Mark, who I have had the delight to work for many times over the years, and now class as friends.

They were featured in my *For the Love of Pets* book about their dog Bonzo. Here are a few words which are now relevant to this one...

When we did a reading with Jackie, following the loss of our beautiful boy Bonzo, not only did it give us great comfort, but so many other amazing things also led on from the reading.

In our reading, Bonzo told us that we were looking for a picture to put beside his urn. He said that he thought that his picture was going to be beautiful and should be it should be one with him lying down with his legs crossed! Now whilst Bonzo always used to cross his legs, we could only find one photo of him like that and it wasn't a great one of him.

In the end, we had to enlist the help of a family member who managed to edit a lovely photo of him lying down to show him with his legs crossed. He then also put this photo into a beautiful landscape shot in the Lake District which was one of Bonzo's favourite holiday places.

To complete the picture, he added a younger head shot of Bonzo appearing as a ghost in the clouds to depict him looking down over us. We adore it and sure Bonzo would too.

Had Bonzo not suggested such a specific picture of him, the end picture would not have been anywhere near as beautiful. When we sent it over to show Jackie, she immediately asked us if she could use it on the front of this book's cover. We were so delighted, and proud, just as Bonzo is, we are sure.

Apart from the picture, he gave us another suggestion; for me (Kathy) to write a poem for the retired greyhound memorial site, instead of a write up that I had had intended to. Now, I am by no means a writer, and definitely no poet, but I gave it a go and used the title 'Our Black Prince' as he suggested the title. I am proud of the words that appeared on the paper which I still can't believe actually came from me., and guess I did get some 'Heavenly' help…

Our Beautiful Black Prince

Bonzo how we love you so

We miss you like you'll never know

You got us back out on our feet

And simply made our life complete

You were a beauty, people used to say

Came 3rd most handsome one such day

You had such presence when you were here

Calling you 'Prince' would've been a great idea!

But to us you were 'Bonzo' and always will stay

Deep in our hearts forever each day

It's rare a dog as special as you

Comes along and breaks your heart in two

You made us laugh, you made us smile

But we had you for too short a while

How we wish you didn't have to go

We will love you forever and hope you know

Our time with you was the best time ever

Leaving memories in our hearts to treasure

Goodbye sweet friend for now we say

Until we meet again one day

You will find more about Bonzo, and a true Angel, further on in this book. I hope these stories touch your heart and really show you that we never 'die' – we just move to another dimension to join up with those who have gone before us.

Rod and his cat Tosca

The Chicago Herald newspaper has a well-known slogan: 'If your mother says she loves you, check it out!' This is my approach to the world of spirit; everything has to be verified. However, I have been extraordinarily successful talking to 'people' who have passed over through utilising Inter-dimensional Trans-Communication (ITC), a form of Electronic Voice Phenomenon. Humans, I knew, were fully conscious upon leaving their bodies. When my companion of 17 years died, though, I was lost, for Tosca was a beautiful tabby cat. How on earth would I contact her?

Well, I did what everyone does nowadays when they have a question they can't answer – I turned to Google. And that is where I found Jackie's website. Perhaps contacting Tosca was possible after all. It was certainly worth a try.

Tosca came into my life on 20 November 2002, the day after seeing Puccini's opera Tosca in Birmingham. She was just eight weeks old when I fetched her from a lady whose cat had had six kittens. Tosca was the last one not spoken for. I fell in love with her the moment I saw her and we were virtually inseparable for the next 16 years and 11 months. I'm a writer by trade and work from home, so Tosca was always there. The only time we spent apart was when I went on holiday. I recall going on a longer than usual holiday back in 2008 to India, and when I returned Tosca dashed out of the house, along a low wall next to the car, and leapt into my arms! For me, this is one of life's most treasured memories.

When I had to take her to the vet on 20 October 2019, therefore, it was incredibly painful. But she wasn't eating, wasn't drinking, and was obviously in discomfort. Her kidneys were giving out, and the vet told me she would only have another few days at the most. It was distressing, but euthanasia was the only option.

I was distraught when I returned home; knowing that life was eternal didn't help at all! I needed to contact Tosca to see if she had transited okay and was now happy and out of any pain she was feeling.

When Jackie called me, it was just 12 days after Tosca had passed, and I must admit there were a few butterflies when the reading began. The first thing I was told was "Tosca is giving you primroses. She is very insistent." I had no idea why I was being given primroses. However, a couple of hours later, I decided to look up the symbolic meaning of the primrose and discovered it stood for 'eternal love'. This certainly brought a tear to my eye, as the last thing I ever said to Tosca was "I will love you forever." The first thing she had said to me through Jackie, was the last thing I said to her. That is almost too beautiful for words.

Jackie then told me that Tosca liked to be with me – she followed me around a bit like a dog really – and was very much a home girl. This is 100% accurate. She did follow me around the house and had very little interest in going outside, usually just venturing into the back garden for 10 minutes on a sunny day. Tosca always had access to the great outdoors, but she just never bothered too much. She was the ultimate 'home girl'.

Tosca then told me it was just me and her, a quiet life, although she said she never objected to visitors! Again, this hit the nail on the head. Mostly, it was just Tosca and I. It is true, I am married, but I met my wife later in life when we both had homes of our own, and we've kept it that way. It sounds strange to some people, but it works for us. So, yes, Tosca was right when she said it was just 'me and her'.

She also said she enjoyed lying on the settee with me, which she did. Her purr could be heard at a hundred yards some evenings while we were reading or listening to music together, although she walked out if I was playing Shostakovich. I had a cat who was a music critic!

Jackie came up with the names 'Mary', then 'Grace'. I said that I had no clue about either of them and she said just to note them anyway as sometimes they become apparent. The very next day, I opened a box of DVDs and books I was planning to take to the local hospice shop in order to add a couple more items. Lying on the top was a South American film by the title of 'Maria Full of Grace'. Maria is, of course, Spanish for Mary, so the two names were staring up at me on the front of a single DVD! Amazing.

Next, Tosca talked about when she passed, saying that she never looked or felt really old (which she didn't); it was just that the wind had gone out of her sails. She did point out that she still had a lot of her own teeth left though, adding proudly that in the last few days she still used her tray and there were no 'accidents'. She said, her passing over was easy; her breathing just slowly stopped. Tosca said she knew I had taken her to the vet to be kind to her and felt me stroking her as she moved from this realm to the next. She finished by saying that she was glad that we were able to say goodbye in that way because she would only have lived for another three or four days and it wouldn't have been pleasant.

Tosca then explained that she hardly ever saw a vet in her life and was lucky because she had a life of luxury. That was undoubtedly true; she visited a vet a total of just four times over 17 years. She was a good eater too, she added, saying she loved her food and never missed a bit! No argument there. Tosca ate well. She was given the best food I could source (often fresh fish) and licked her plate clean. Mealtimes were her favourite part of the day. She even told Jackie about the cupboard where her food was stored!

Tosca then relayed a couple of facts that underlined she was still very much alive in spirit. She said I have a lot of books, and that reading is an excellent form of escapism for me. I probably have too many books, so that is certainly true. Jackie said she was slightly confused by the next picture Tosca was giving her. She said, 'It was like you were moving a clock face, which is odd as they do not move, do they? I explained that I knew exactly what Tosca was trying to convey... I have a clock that I pick up regularly. Around 15 years ago, I purchased an old Soviet clock at an antique fair, and every day or so it needs winding. It also needs the time correcting, as it tends to lose about five minutes each day, hence the moving on the clock face. Tosca said that when I wind it now, I will always think of her. Jackie said she was calling it a 'timely think'.

Tosca then went on to tell me about a rug she played on as a kitten, lifting up and kicking the corners. She said I still have that rug, which I do. It was one of her favourite places to lie down and chill, right up until a couple of days before she passed.

Her memories of her time with me also include sitting in a conservatory and lounging in the sun. She said I could see her whenever I returned home. This is an interesting point because, unlike most conservatories, mine is at the front of the house, so when I walked up the path to the front door, I could often see her asleep in the sun on one of her favourite chairs.

Tosca also mentioned the lady who used to look after her when I went on holiday, saying that the lady spoke gently to her, which I know she always did. She also said that there was a musical link that that lady and I would know about. As already mentioned, the day before I picked her up as a kitten, I went to see Tosca, the opera, and that lady was with me. It was the two of us that decided on Tosca's name.

The final statement was wonderful and life-affirming. Tosca said that she came into my life as a guide and that sometimes she will still visit me on the settee. She said her life was a natural full circle and that she was very lucky. Tosca concluded by saying that I now have the freedom to do different things and that she understood that looking after her was a big responsibility. It's a responsibility I wish I still had, but hearing from Tosca has made a big difference to my life and wellbeing. It's never 'easy' but knowing that she's okay and that I'll see her again makes it 'easier'.

I have to say that the intense joy that results from the complete realisation of the actual presence and identity of a so-called 'dead' animal companion; of their independent activity; of their unchanged characteristics – that they are genuinely still living, thinking, remembering, loving, and happy and that they are just themselves. This is really needs to be experienced to be entirely understood.

Jackie has a rare and unique gift, and I can't thank her enough for allowing to me hear from Tosca. I know I shall see Tosca gain, but Jackie has helped me realise that she is still around anyway ... I just need to 'listen'.

*****

Kirsty and her dog Benson

After all my life wanting a dog and nagging my parents for one, the day had finally arrived. I was 13 years old and had finished school for the day, I remember being so beyond excited it was the best feeling. It was time to go and see the two puppies that we had found advertised in the local newspaper, two Staffordshire Bull Terriers.

We arrived at the owner's house and straight-away one puppy ran over to me and wouldn't leave me alone – he was so lovely. I was told he was the cheeky one out of the two. His name was Brock. He was pure black with a white star on his chest, such a beautiful little puppy. He was a daddy's boy the owners told me as he used to really annoy his mum with his extremely hyper and playful behaviour. I fell in love with him and instantly knew he was the one I wanted and not sure who chose who? I scooped him up in my arms and we left I couldn't believe I had a puppy after all this time of wanting one. I was so happy.

The poor little thing was understandably scared; he cried at night for the first couple of weeks. He was poorly too as he had quite a nasty sickness bug. My mum stayed up with him through the night to make sure he was okay. After a while he soon settled in and when I woke up in the morning, I would race downstairs to see him. He was as happy to see me, as

I was to see him – he became my best friend. I changed his name from Brock to Benson as it suited him much better.

He taught me what it was really like to love. I would give him a thousand cuddles and kisses every day. We had so much fun together and I would take him over to our local field and he would run and run and play with all the other dogs around. He loved it. He became a massive part of our family and although my mum wasn't a dog lover, it was clear to see she felt for him exactly what I did. We had so many compliments about him from people when we used to take him to different places. We even had people ask to buy him and breed from him, of course the answer to both was 'No' as he was our baby boy. Every Saturday we used to walk him around our town and everyone got to know him and love him. Benson adored it as he got so much fuss. One day I remember when he cocked his leg up a lady's shopping trolley as we walked past whilst she was waiting at the bus stop. Mum and I were mortified and we hurried him along, luckily the lady didn't see what happened, and being a young girl then, it made me giggle. He was always doing things to embarrass us like when there was a football match and once he ran in to the middle of the pitch and ran off with their football – he was a little monkey.

He was a beautiful boy inside and out. One day we took him to a local dog show and he came first in the 'best-looking dog'. I was so proud of him. We had so many lovely days together leaving me with so many happy memories. Benny boy, as I called him, was the happiest dog ever. He had tonnes of energy, he was boisterous and very playful and I loved this about him. I taught him to sit, shake paw, lie down and to kiss me. 'Kiss' was our special thing. I would randomly say 'kiss' and he would come over and kiss me. He was one in a million, so gentle, friendly and kind hearted. I had a rabbit at the time also, called Frisky and he used to bully Benson! He would chase him around the garden and bite his legs and never once did Benny retaliate, not even a little growl.

Everyone knew how truly adorable Benson was which is also what Jackie brought up in his communication. The vets loved him and he was so well behaved; he used to walk in to greet the vet so happy with the waggiest tail. In the reading, Jackie mentioned he was a cheeky boy who had a mind of his own and talked about when he used to open and stick his head in the kitchen cupboards – it was always the biscuit cupboard, needless to say. He always used to greet everyone with something in his mouth, no matter if it was big or small; he was so funny. He brought so much happiness into our lives; we couldn't imagine our life without him.

My boyfriend bought me another dog, a Shitzu and I called her Princess. From day one of introducing them, Benson was so soft and gentle with her even though the same can't be said about her! She used to boss him around and even though we had owned him seven years previous to having her, he allowed her to boss him around in what was really his house. This showed how lovely natured he was, he was a big softy.

My sister had a baby, my niece called Tiger-lily, and Benson loved being with her. He used to sit there while she was prodding his ears or sticking her hands in his mouth and she even used to crawl into bed with him. He would snuggle up to her, and they would both have a sleep. He didn't have a bad bone in his body; he was the most loyal dog, a real family dog he was perfect. Even my neighbours loved him as he very rarely barked, such a good boy. (The lack of barking was something Jackie picked up on. In her words, 'he wasn't a barky dog'.) He was such a character; he made us all smile every single day, which was great as sadly my mum had begun her battle with ovarian cancer. He used to comfort her throughout her illness. He made us all happy when we were sad and going through hard times he was our rock. He used to sniff at my mum's stomach – he knew something wasn't right.

One day mum was stroking Benson and she felt lumps in his throat/neck area. I felt ever so guilty that I hadn't been the one to notice it. We stayed positive as we were convinced it would be an infection that had spread from his ears, as he always suffered from ear infections. Nevertheless, we rang the vets straight away and booked him in for an appointment that same day. The vets called us in and she felt all around his throat/neck area and almost instantly said he had lymphoma (cancer of the immune system) and my heart sank. My mum howled as she sobbed and asked so many questions, the main one being, can it be treated? How long does he have? Etc. etc. The vet said he can have chemotherapy and steroids to prolong his life but even with the treatment we are looking at two to eight months. My mum broke her heart even more. I'm not sure how but I managed to keep it together. We walked out of the vets in shock, as we got into the car outside I broke down. Poor Benson didn't know what was going on and my heart felt like it had been shattered into a million pieces.

He started his treatment soon after and still Benson was happy to see everyone at the vets even knowing he was about to be poked and prodded. (Jackie said Benson was so brave throughout his illness) and he truly was the bravest boy in the world. He tried to carry on like his normal self but I could tell he was in pain – this was unbearable to watch. After a few sessions of chemo, his tumours had shrunk they were barely there at all. I had my old Benny back I felt so relieved I started searching the Internet for hours at a time for foods and natural remedies that would help. I was adamant he would be cured.

Sadly this was short lived and we noticed his tumours had come back once again and my heart just sank. We spoke with the vets and asked if anything else could be done. We didn't care about the cost and they offered to have him transferred to a veterinary university where they could try different medications. Although it was a couple of hours away from our home, without hesitation, we said, yes. I just wanted him around for as long as possible. My parents knew how much I loved him and would try anything. We took him for a couple of visits down there and they tried some new tablet. Sadly there was no positive change so he was booked in for his third appointment where he was going to have radiotherapy. Unfortunately he didn't make it.

On Saturday the 25th of August 2012 he went outside in the garden for a wee, lay down on the ground and passed away. I was down the stables with my boyfriend at the time as I have a horse called Cuddles. I had a call from my dad saying, 'Sorry darling but you need to come home Benson has passed away'. I cried uncontrollably and my boyfriend drove me home.

Benson was lying in his little bed that my dad had put him in for when I got home – my world completely felt crushed. He was my everything. I was devastated. I chose to take him to a really nice pet crematorium to have him privately cremated. Saying goodbye was just the hardest thing, I cut pieces of his fur off and keep them in my locket necklace.

Jackie said that I had had a dream about him. I told her it was that same night that he passed away he came back to me in my dream. I usually can never remember my dreams but this one was so clear and so real. I could hear him running up the stairs to my bedroom and he ran over to me so full of energy, healthy looking and he was really happy. He was a younger version of himself just what he used to look like. Whenever I think of this dream it makes me so happy as I know it was him coming back to me to show me he is free of pain and happy.

My mum was absolutely heartbroken over Benson and with her being so poorly herself it made me worry, I was right to worry. Sadly on the Thursday the 30th of August, just five days after losing my gorgeous Benny boy, my mum passed away. She too had lost her battle with cancer just like Benson had. I thought my heart couldn't break any more but the pain and ache I felt is too hard to explain. I had lost my two loves, my rocks within the space of five days of each other. My whole life changed.

I tried searching for comfort and this is when I found Jackie via the internet. I can't thank her enough as she has proved to me by everything she told me from Benson, that there really is life after death. I know for certain that my mum and Benson are watching over me and always will do. Jackie truly believes Benson came through to me and for my mum as well. I was totally shocked when Benson passed a message from her saying that she is no longer worrying about her weight like she did. It might seem strange that a person in spirit would mention this, but I knew exactly why. At the beginning of her treatment she gained a lot through the steroids and the last few months of her life she lost an awful lot. I now know because of Benson and Jackie that my mum is happy and healthy again, just like he is too. The warm tingly feelings I got whilst talking to Jackie were really lovely. She is a truly gifted lady and I will be forever be thankful to her.

*****

Louise and her Horse Wiz

After I lost my beloved horse Wiz I feel honoured (and know he does too) to be able to share his story here. He was my best friend, partner and soulmate and for 23 years – I was so blessed to share his life.

Ever since I can recall, I loved horses and started asking for a pony when I was four years old! When I was older, I started going to a local riding school as my Nan would send me the money for my lessons. I made the most of it and would stay on to help out as I loved being near horses every chance I got. I knew I desperately wanted a horse of my own but aged 15 I realised it wasn't going to happen and decided I wouldn't go again until I could realise my dream. I was 31 when I started riding again, and this time there was no stopping me! I was determined to find 'my horse' and took stable management courses to refresh my dated knowledge and started looking for my 1st horse.

On May 19th 1994, my life changed forever when I met Wiz. He was a three-year-old chocolate brown Connemara / Thoroughbred cross that had just been backed to ride. I loved him immediately and although he didn't make things easy, I earned his trust and we soon had the most amazing bond. I told him many times throughout the years how lucky I was to have him, and how glad he was born so he could be my 1st horse

We learnt together and had amazing times doing just about everything. We always loved to gallop and jump and that usually meant at top speed. Cross-country was our favourite and he was a fabulous jumper.

In 1996 I was very lucky to have him and our other horse (chosen by Wiz but for my husband to ride) at our home with nine acres for them. Life was so wonderful and hearing him answer me every morning when I shouted to him as I was getting his feed ready – it was the best sound ever. I enjoyed his company more than anybody's and always loved chatting to him when it was just the two of us hacking (riding) out and about.

I always felt Wiz and I were very close and knew each other inside out; I trusted him with my life. He simply knew my thoughts and understood everything I said. I loved my boy more than the world!

When I saw an article in our local newspaper about animal psychic Jackie Weaver, I knew I wanted her to speak to Wiz. He was nineteen now but to me he was still a three-year-old and the same beautiful fun horse he'd always been. I sent Jackie a photo of Wiz with his age and how long I had had him and she booked my appointment. I was so excited and couldn't wait to hear what he would have to say.

Jackie rang at the agreed time and she immediately made me feel at ease as she explained how it worked, it was a three-way conversation through her. The 1st thing Wiz said was, "I am divine" and I knew it was definitely him! He told her I had known what he would look like before I met him and that was very true! I did and told her why. Many other wonderful things that confirmed to me it was him: She asked me why was he showing her his top lip and I knew straight away he was giving her a 'Wiz kiss'; he did this brilliantly along with shaking hands (well hooves) and opening gates when I asked him to. She said when he neighed to me (he did it every time he saw me) he was saying "Hi mum". This made perfect sense because every time I saw him I shouted "Hi Wiz" so we were greeting each other as friends do.

He told her he felt the same way about me (I always told him how much I loved him) and I understood this because he wasn't one for showing his feelings, at the end of the reading he told me not to worry as he 'would make old bones'. I thought that was lovely but also made sure I reminded him of what he'd said over the next few years. (Jackie did say at the time, she of course could not guarantee this but if they say it, she passes it on and hoped it would be as said.)

The years passed and Wiz honestly was 'my life'. I didn't want to go away on holiday (not even overnight) as I so looked forward to seeing him several times every day. It made me so happy every time I heard his voice. We still enjoyed riding about and he looked amazing. Aged 21, Wiz started showing signs of stiffness in his right back leg and my vet said it was most likely arthritis and we managed it with pain relief, joint supplements and 'Bio flow' magnetic boots. He was still top dog in the herd and they all knew he was the boss.

By the time he was 24, he would often struggle to get up if he lay on his right side so, even when having a roll, he would try to get up from his left side. This problem was not unexpected due to an old injury when he was a four-year-old. (One day, when his field companion had been taken out, he galloped downhill to follow them but the gate had already been shut and found he could not stop in time due to the mud. He tried to jump it and unfortunately got his front legs over but caught his back leg causing dreadful injuries.)

He was very accident-prone throughout his lifetime and had stitches and staples many times. My 'warrior horse' always bounced back but now his old injuries were starting to take their toll. I told him we had done everything over the years and he didn't need to gallop or jump anymore. I didn't mind because I was old now too but we could still do it in our dreams instead.

Just after Christmas, Wiz who was now 26 had several bouts of colic. (Colic is a type of stomach-ache which in a horse, especially as physically they cannot be sick, it is very painful and can be very serious.) The vet came each time and he would recover, although it took longer each time. I was very worried and just couldn't imagine my life without him. On March 3rd he had very bad torsion colic (twisted gut) and this time was different – I could see in his face he had had enough and was obviously in severe pain. The vet examined him and said there was nothing they could do as the cord of a tumour was wrapped round very tight and he would have to be put to sleep. I felt dazed and couldn't believe what I was hearing. Wiz was my whole life and I always told him he couldn't leave me. Friends who had known us both always said they dreaded this day for me because they knew how much I loved him. I kissed him goodbye, thanked him for every second I'd had with him and he passed so peacefully and with such courage and dignity. Even at the end my boy was so brave and I was so proud of him. I felt completely dazed and empty; nothing seemed real.

I knew I had to hear from him and make sure he was alright so I messaged Jackie to ask her how soon I could speak to him as I'd never gone a single day without talking to him in life. She sent me a lovely message saying she was very sorry for my loss. She suggested if I could wait two weeks for him to settle and adjust to spirit life, and for me to be strong enough to have a conversation with him, that would be better. These were the hardest two weeks of my life. She gave me time and date and I waited (impatiently) for her call. Jackie rang at my allotted time and just as the last time I felt at ease and she connected with my wonderful boy.

He told her how 'that day' he had gone down in the field and couldn't get up this time, she said because of a problem with his right hind leg. (Previously I hadn't told her about the accident when he was four.) He said that he could see me talking to a very life-like picture of him (very true) and he could see it too. He said, "It is as if I'm really there!" He then made us both laugh saying that he could sit on my bed if I wanted him to, as he could be simply anywhere. I loved that! Jackie said the next part was strange and she'd never heard a horse say it before… he told her that he used to dream, and in his dreams he would run! I knew exactly what this meant; As Wiz was no longer able to gallop around like he used to, I used to say to him that he could still run in his dreams. This was something between Wiz and I. Nobody else ever knew this. Once again I realised just how amazing Jackie is.

He talked about his passing and how inside a 'string like something' had wrapped over his gut. His description of his colic was spot on and Jackie couldn't have known this. He then mentioned a weanling (foal weaned from its mum) crying, and horse called Ella. I couldn't make any connection with weanling, or Ella, but it is was what Jackie had repeated from him, so I wrote it down. He asked about the little grey pony (his companion Eddie) and asked, 'Is he okay without me?' We assured him he was and Wiz went on to tell us many details about Eddie and his quirks perfectly. I was in no doubt, as in the previous reading, that I was hearing from my wonderful boy and even though now in spirit he hadn't changed a bit. He said he'd loved everything we did together, such fun and that we were partners - so true, we most certainly were.

He ended the reading by showing Jackie a vision of him blitzing off up a hill and said, 'This is me now.' I loved knowing he was happy and fit once again and that was so him blasting everywhere whenever he could.

A few weeks after my reading with Jackie a weanling arrived at the yard in a very sad and poor state. I asked her new owner what her name was and she said 'Ella'. Well, you could have knocked me down with a feather – this was the weanling Wiz had mentioned in the spirit reading! Although I had never doubted anything either he, or Jackie said, I was completely blown away! A few months on and this young horse, who now looks amazing, and is definitely not crying and sad anymore. She has fantastic people who love and look after her so well. She is a very special horse with such character and I can totally see why Wiz would know and care about her.

I still talk to Wiz every day and will always miss him but Jackie gave me peace of mind and I know he is still my Wiz. In his clever words, he explained, " It's only my body that has gone but my soul remains." Jackie is a wonderful lady with the most amazing gift in communicating with animals whether living or in spirit. I will always be grateful to her for giving me the comfort of hearing from him and knowing he's still around.

I have been truly blessed to have shared 23 years with my boy and have known such love and friendship. I know he will be very proud to be immortalised in one of Jackie's books, but knowing him and his high self-opinion, I'm sure he expected nothing less.

*****

Caroline and her Cat Tewa

It was in the Summer of 2008 that I first met my beautiful cat, Tewa. My husband Steve and I had just lost our precious cat, Twiggy after we had to have her put to sleep at the age of 17. We decided that the house just wasn't the same without a feline presence so we started our search for a cat who needed a good home. We ended up with two cats; Zuni, a big black gentle bear of a cat aged 18 months and Tewa a grey tabby with the most beautiful markings, aged 1 year. Their owner, who had had them since they were kittens, was just about to move to a flat in Edinburgh and it wouldn't have been a suitable environment for cats, so very reluctantly they decided to rehome them. Their names, Zuni and Tewa, were unusual and we learned that they are Pueblo Indian tribe names.

We were told that Zuni was a very soft affectionate cat despite his size, and that Tewa was very naughty and had a habit of licking your nose then biting it when you least expected it!

They soon settled into their new home with us. They were very independent of each other and led separate lives. Zuni was quite happy to stay close to home while Tewa would wander off and do her own thing. She was always the one who at times would go missing overnight or would be away from home for hours on end and I was always worrying about her. She was such a confident little thing and utterly fearless and could be very naughty at times (we called her a little Minx) but at the same time, she was so loveable.

She used to manage to get on to the roof of our bungalow, have a wander around then couldn't work out how to get down. We used to have to hold up a laundry basket for her to climb into in order that she could be rescued.

At one time she went missing overnight. I hadn't slept a wink and couldn't wait until daylight so that I could get out to look for her properly. I called her name the next day and I was so overjoyed to hear her meowing! It seemed to be coming from next-door's garden. I had a look around but just couldn't see her. Her crying seemed to be coming from up above and I realized that she must be in next door's loft! I had to phone my neighbour at his work to ask him to come home and set her free. He wasn't best pleased, especially when she managed to get into their loft again the next night and woke him up at two in the morning exploring it! It turned out that there was a hole in their garage that lead into the loft which she had found. They blocked the hole up and it didn't happen again.

She used to come and waken me in the middle of the night demanding food after she had been out on her travels. There was always food down for her but she wanted me to get up and give her fresh! If I didn't get up, she would stand on my pillow and bite, pull and shake my hair until I did. A very spoiled lady indeed!

As I mentioned above, there were times when she would disappear overnight or for hours on end. I would be so worried and then she'd just appear through her cat flap and look at me as if to say, 'What's all the fuss about and can I have some food please?' She was a very vocal cat and had a beautiful high-pitched meow too – one you really could not ignore.

A week ago as I was about to leave for work, a neighbour came to the door and said there was a dead cat outside her house. My worst nightmare. I just knew it would be Tewa. She had been hit by a car and thankfully it looked like her death had been instant. I was just devastated and the tears are falling fast again as I write this. We buried her in the garden in a beautiful box. I wrote a letter to tell her how much I loved her and how much I would miss her and put that in with her along with a small green pompom that she loved playing football with. We planted a stunning red rose bush called 'Love Lasts Forever' on her grave which will flower on the anniversary of her passing every year.

I felt so grief stricken at having lost my little princess. I couldn't stop crying. I found Jackie Weaver's website and downloaded some of her books. Reading people's experiences of Jackie's spirit readings really helped and I decided to contact her to arrange a reading for myself and Tewa

I sent Jackie a photo of Tewa along with her name; how old she was when she passed; the date of her passing and how long I had owned her for. Jackie sent me a lovely reply, saying that she was so sorry to hear about Tewa and mentioned that she was such a pretty little girl. A date and time for my phone reading was arranged.

On the day Jackie was to call, I was so nervous. I couldn't settle to do anything. Just beforehand, I lit a candle for Tewa which I had been doing every day and I had a photo of her beside me. I also had paper and pen at the ready so that I could scribble down everything that was said. Jackie mentioned in her email that some animals are more forthcoming than others but I felt that, even if Tewa didn't come forward, it would be therapeutic to just even chat to Jackie.

She called at 3pm on the dot and within seconds I felt so relaxed with her. She was so friendly and easy to talk to and it almost felt like I had known her for years. There was no need for me to have felt so nervous beforehand. Jackie went on to explain that although animals have passed, they are still living in spirit and they talk to her as if they are still living as they are, just in a different place.

The first thing that Jackie asked was if we had a small black cat and yes, as well as Zuni (who is a *big* black cat) we have Sharples who turned up at our house as a stray a few years ago, and we kept him. A lovely little character who worships Zuni and follows him around everywhere!

To my delight, Jackie managed to make contact with Tewa just before she called me. Tewa said, 'I lived on the lighter side of life, carefree and affectionate with it.' I couldn't agree more. That statement described her character very accurately.

She added, 'I never went far', and showed Jackie a vision of her lying in a flowerbed. To be honest, I never really knew how far she went. Maybe when she had been gone for hours she was just next-door or across the road relaxing in a garden. We don't have any flowerbeds but some of the neighbours do.

Tewa said that the neighbours knew her. Since her passing, I have found out that she was a regular visitor at a few of the houses nearby. I hadn't realized that before. She was a friendly little thing and loved to be admired so I'm not surprised.

Tewa said that she knew the hedgehog! This made Jackie smile and she said that it was such a lovely thing for Tewa to mention; The week after we lost her, we had a hedgehog wandering around our garden and we were told by the neighbours that it visits them too, so how wonderful that Tewa would have seen it too.

Jackie then went on to talk about Tewa's passing. I'd been fine up until that point and then the tears came. Jackie was so understanding about this though and put my mind at rest that Tewa didn't suffer. She said that her passing was very fast; Gone; Hit on the Head; Knew nothing; Out like a light. This was so comforting and at the same time amazing as Jackie didn't know the circumstances of Tewa's passing and she did indeed sustain a head injury. She showed Jackie that she was fine in spirit and wanted me to be reassured of this. That was so wonderful to hear.

Tewa went on to say that she was very confident and always made herself at home. She would lounge about on the settee and would do her own thing. Very true. She was a very independent lady and very bossy at the same time. The photograph that I sent to Jackie shows Tewa as being very regal and well behaved. Jackie said that when she looked at the photograph she got the impression of Tewa dipping her head down as if to say, 'Kiss me if you want' and 'I'm in charge!' which was so her. Jackie got Tewa's character exactly right.

Tewa went on to say, 'I was extremely happy with my life. You gave me everything; attention and food and I was very clever and managed to get food from elsewhere too!' It felt so good to hear this. I absolutely adore my cats and it feels so good to know that I made her happy. I laughed about the food from elsewhere though – I hadn't realized that others were feeding her too. She was always so slim and trim but the amount of energy she always had would have soon burned up the calories.

Jackie then asked if there was a Ben significant to us? The only Ben I can think of was my mother-in-law's boxer dog who passed away a few years ago. Jackie was shown a dog lying down with his front paws splayed out wide. Afterwards I checked with my mother-in-law and indeed, he did used to lie down in that way with his head between his splayed front paws. Tewa said that they had met up and that very often she bats her paw at him! On the day of Tewa's passing, I visited my father and mother-in-law. My husband Steve was away and I needed some company. I hadn't heard talk of Ben for years but we were talking about him that day and then Jackie mentioning him in the reading seemed more than coincidence.

Tewa added, 'There's nothing to fear up here. Completely safe environment and very busy with animals and people.' She then went on to say that in life everything was on her own terms and she'd suddenly turn around to us and give us the impression of her saying, 'Right I'm off now!' Again, a very accurate description of her character.

Tewa said that she would keep a wide berth from the little black cat. Again this was true; Sharples sometimes used to lie in wait to ambush her when she wasn't expecting it and she got most indignant about it. She also said that she wasn't into fighting. Again, very true. She used to steer clear of other cats in the neighbourhood. However, when Sharples ambushed her they used to bat each other with their paws like they were in a little boxing match. Tewa used to yowl as if she was trying to get him into trouble.

She mentioned that Sharples made strange noises. This is so true. I have never met a cat like Sharples before. He's a lovely little character and really does make the strangest of sounds. Tewa mentioned that Sharples darts around a lot like he is always in a hurry and this again was very accurate. Tewa then made Jackie and I laugh when she described Sharples as 'A Wee Belter'. I was not sure if she was referring to their little boxing matches or if she thought he was a great puss despite him regularly ambushing her. Tewa then showed Jackie giving him a pat with her paw.

Tewa said that she wasn't really a lap cat. Again true; She liked to sit on a cushion on Steve's lap at certain times but it was only when she was in the mood.

I mentioned to Jackie that Tewa hadn't been her usual self the evening before she died. Steve especially picked up on this, and had even suggested she seemed a bit down, and maybe we should take her to the vet? She also seemed more affectionate than usual and would let us stroke her for longer. Jackie explained that we all come in with a date to go out and that Tewa would have been spiritually aware that her time was near and would have been guided to lap up affection that night. She wouldn't have known what was going to happen though thankfully.

Tewa went on to say 'I never bit hard I just 'told'!' This was once again very accurate. She was a little minx and if you stroked her for a second too long she would nibble your hand.

I was absolutely stunned by what was said next... Jackie asked if I had an angel ornament and I said 'yes' and then she added that had it seemed it had been taken from its usual place and was being moved around a lot at the moment? The tears came again and I took a minute to contain myself. My friend Hazel, another cat lover, had given me the ornament as a present a few months ago. It was a ceramic figure holding a cat and it had angel wings made out of wire.

Every day since I lost Tewa I have been taking the angel with me to whichever part of the house I happen to be in and lighting a candle for her as a way of having her close. I even took it with me on a trip to Southport a week after Tewa's passing. How could Jackie possibly have known this? It was incredible. Jackie went on to say that Tewa had seen me move the ornament which lets me know that she is with me and watches what I'm doing.

Jackie got the impression that Tewa was an amazing cat and that we had a lovely relationship and I have to say that I always feel very close to my cats and treat them with lots of love and respect. Tewa said that she loved this life and it's wonderful to feel that I played a part in her happiness.

Earlier in the phone call Jackie mentioned that she herself had made a safety garden built for her cat and the peace of mind that it gives her is just fantastic. Although Zuni and Sharples always seem to stay in the garden and are a lot less worry than Tewa was. To be able to keep them away from any possibility of danger would add a wonderful new dimension to cat ownership. Tewa told Jackie that she felt that Zuni and Sharples would be happy with a safety garden but that it wouldn't have suited her.

I felt a certain amount of guilt after losing Tewa thinking that I had kept her safe, and not allowed her to wander so much, would she still be alive now? Tewa actually said to Jackie not to think this way and not to feel 'I should have done this or that...' I like to think that Tewa was thankful for the freedom that we gave her and wouldn't have been happy if that freedom had been restricted in any way. Jackie was kind enough to send me photographs of her safety garden and I am considering how I can adapt our garden in a similar way.

Tewa added that I should tell Zuni and Sharples that the garden is their safe place and they'll understand me. I now tell them this every day and they do seem to be quite content to stay close to home. She said that she has been watching over us and that Zuni and Sharples are fine. They have coped with her passing. Jackie mentioned that animals are very intuitive and they will know that Tewa has gone to the spirit world.

Jackie asked if I had any questions and I was keen to know whether Tewa had met any of our previous cats in Heaven. Jackie said that Tewa had given her the name 'Milky' or 'Malky'? None of our cats had that name but when I mentioned that we had lost a white one a few years ago, Jackie said that's the one. Milky would have been referring to his colour in the same way that we might call a black cat, Blackie.

Tewa then said, 'I can safely go anywhere now. Even through a window. I am my own true self and your home is a haven for love.' How beautiful and special to hear this and how comforting. I mentioned to Jackie that I had been looking on line for rescue cats requiring a home but that in my heart I knew it would upset the harmony in the house. Zuni and Sharples are quite happy as they are and they get on well together. Tewa confirmed this by saying, 'Don't complicate things' and I have decided to take her advice.

Those forty precious minutes talking to Tewa and Jackie absolutely flew past. It was one of the best experiences of my life and I would recommend it to anyone who is grieving over the loss of a pet. Although I am still sad, still crying as I still miss my special lady terribly, I feel so much better and I am convinced that Tewa is now having the most wonderful time in Paradise and I find it so easy to imagine her there. I have always believed in a spirit world and now I am utterly convinced. Jackie is such a special lady. Her gift is incredible and I will be spreading the word and recommending her to others.

Through this experience and through reading Jackie's fascinating books I feel I now have more of an understanding of animals. I speak to Zuni and Sharples all the time and instead of sitting at a PC working for hours on end, I am spending more time with them and giving them much more attention. I appreciate every day with them and I enjoy them. Jackie has made a huge difference to the way I think about my everyday life and what my priorities should be. Thank you so much, Jackie!

Tewa would be extremely proud to appear in one of Jackie's books and I write this as a tribute to her – a very beautiful, dainty, special and unique girl.

*****

Jackie and her dog Millie

Millie was a West Highland Terrier. I always called her 'my little girl'. She came into my life on Thursday 12th April 2012. I never really knew how old she was, but the vet's best guess was around seven years old.

I have always had rescue dogs, and usually liked to rescue the older doggies who are so often overlooked because of their age. A friend called me to tell me of a Westie in dire circumstances who was in the process of being rescued. Would I foster her for a few weeks to get her to a place of safety. I said 'Yes' without hesitation.

A few hours later she walked into my life, well carried to be exact. Her background was that she had been used as a breeding bitch on a puppy farm. After having many litters and unable to produce anymore, she had now outlived her profitable use. Covered with mammary tumours, infected ears and teeth, she had been dumped out onto the street to fend for herself. This poor girl had never been outside of the cage she had been kept in, so she knew nothing of the outside world. How on earth she managed to survive, I will never know.

She was picked up by a passerby, but unfortunately things went from bad to worse for her. Because she had never been inside a house, she hadn't been house trained and was terrified of every single noise. She found herself on the verge of being put back out on the streets again. However, thankfully she was finally rescued and now sat on my sofa, probably wondering what awful things were going to happen to her next. Little did she know, that from the moment she came to me, she was at last safe. She was to become my Millie (as I named her) and it turned out, she was never going to be just a foster dog; she was to be with me for the rest of her days.

The first priority was to get her checked over by the vet. Within a few days she was booked in to have her mammary tumours removed, some teeth taken out and spayed, all of which she got through with flying colours. As the days and weeks passed, it became apparent that she wasn't used to being touched or stroked. But very slowly she began to trust me, and she began to venture from underneath the table in the lounge, her place of safety. I would carry her outside to toilet, and she'd run straight back in and hide.

The first milestone was when she plucked up the courage to walk into the garden for the first time on her own. This was a proud mummy moment for me and I'm not ashamed to say I cried. Every day after that, she'd make little steps forward surprising me every time with her courage and tenacity. Simple things that most dog owners would take for granted, were massive steps forward for my little girl Millie. She was afraid of any noise, afraid of the rain, of little insects in the garden, you name it, she was scared of it.

Over the months, she became more accepting of everyday life. She was never completely at ease, but began to cope in the best way she could. She began to trust me and soon spent every night sleeping on my bed. I did everything I could to make her life as comfortable as possible. I was never able to put a lead on her and take her for a walk as this proved too much for her. However, she would pad around the back garden and even began to take a keen interest in the squirrels which frequented the garden. She would take huge delight in chasing them, knowing of course she couldn't catch them.

She became my shadow and wherever I was, in the house or garden, she would be by my side. This was hugely humbling for me, knowing how she had been treated before, but this didn't stop her from wanting to love and protect me. She didn't bark for the first six months, and I assumed she just didn't bark. One day she heard a sudden noise and let out a loud bark which nearly made me jump two feet in the air, but it made me laugh and cry at the same time, with such pride. How much this little girl had changed in just six months.

Day by day, her little personality started to shine through. I noticed that the apple tree I have in the garden was losing fruit. Then I realised that Millie was either nudging the tree or waiting for the apples to fall off. Then she would carry the apple around the garden for days, nibbling bits off. It would take her about a week to nibble most of it away, after all she only had a few teeth! Millie's great love in life was her food. There were times when I thought she was asleep, so I would go into the kitchen for something to eat. A few seconds later I'd look down, and there she would be, staring up at me, eagerly awaiting any titbits coming her way. She also used to love lying in front of the log fire in the winter months.

Four years on, and in May 2016 she developed a cough. The vet diagnosed heart disease. I was devastated. Millie had struggled so much and had, against all the odds, come through it all. She was put on medication, and at first the cough disappeared and she seemed to show no signs of the heart problem. But as Christmas 2016 came and went, she started to slow down. She stopped following me into the garden, but would prefer to watch me out of the window. By November of that year, I arranged for a home visit by my vet, who told me he didn't think Millie would make Christmas. I was devastated, so decided to give Millie her Christmas presents and treats early. But she astounded me, the vet and everyone else, and we had a lovely Christmas together, which involved me going out and getting more treats and presents to replace the ones she had already enjoyed!

Things took a turn for the worse at the beginning of March 2018, she became very tired and started to refuse her food. Seeing her very rapid decline, I knew the dreaded time had come to say goodbye to my little girl. I arranged for the vet to attend our home and on Wednesday 14th March 2018 at 14.10 pm, Millie passed peacefully away, with me by her side, gently stroking her and telling her that I loved her.

In the days that passed, I needed to know that Millie was safe and I found Jackie Weaver's website. I booked a reading with her for Friday 23rd March at 1.30 pm.

Jackie rang me, immediately putting me at ease, telling me what to expect by way of the reading. Jackie began by describing Millie as a gentle, unassuming girl and Millie saying the words 'puppy farm'. I knew straight away that Jackie had my Millie there with her. Millie made me laugh by saying to Jackie that despite having been on a puppy farm, 'It didn't ruin my looks though!'

Jackie went on to describe how Millie had a cough and that she had passed over with a heart condition. All of which was correct, as Millie's first symptoms were a cough. Millie told Jackie that she had said goodbye to me in a beautiful and serene way. She said that she had blossomed when she came to me and her little personality came out and she felt safe. Millie explained that when I went to work, she didn't panic or worry, she just went to sleep until I came home. Millie described how she would lay her head on her toys when she went to sleep – it was adorable. Jackie told me that Millie kept saying that she was safe, and that she wanted me to know that. I explained to Jackie that this was the main reason I needed a reading to connect with her to know that she was safe.

Millie described how I would always call her, 'My little girl' and that I was very protective over her. She talked about how I liked to keep her nice and soft and well groomed and not like she used to be, all matted and in knots. This was correct, as I used to have a dog groomer come to the house to do her so she wouldn't be too stressed out. Millie said that within the last two or three days I had put up a picture of her. This was so right as I had just put up a framed pencil drawing of Millie in my bedroom. Millie went on to say that I had lights near the picture. Again this was correct, as I had put a small tree with lights on it by her picture to shine next to her.

Millie told Jackie how she was destined to come to me, and that we had a real partnership. Jackie said Millie was showing her a card of a Westie with a hat on with a bobble to one side. I told Jackie that I couldn't think of one at that moment, but would keep an eye out for it. A few days later, I was in my loft and straightaway found some Christmas cards that I had kept, and there was the card! It was exactly as Jackie had described it.

Millie explained it wasn't too early for me to get another dog and went on to describe that the dog would be small and rough coated and younger than Millie had been when she came to me. Millie said, look what you did for me! Millie finished by saying, she wanted to let me know that she feels so lucky to have been with me and that we are a part of each other's soul and that she wants me to smile and be happy.

Having my reading with Jackie has given me complete reassurance that my little girl is safe in Heaven, and is with me always. My reading gave me confirmation that I did my very best for her that I could to make up for the life she had before. For Millie's life story to be published, means that for her and the many rescue animals who have finally found the loving homes they so richly deserve, and that there can be a happy ever after. Until we meet again my little girl. Xx

*****

Mollie the Cat...

The title of this story is different in its style to the others, and that is because this is a different type of story. I have the delight and honour to have such wonderful and kind clients, Michael and Pearl. They

have given such love and a wonderful home to many cats, even to rescue cats, and to some who never thought they would have a home to call their own again. Some were elderly, some classed as mean, but just turned out to be scared. I know this because I have talked to many of them over the years, starting with Oliver who introduced us, so to speak. You will find a story of theirs later on in this book. I was so touched when Pearl, out of the blue, sent this story to me. It is not about our communication at all but what their darling Molly cat channelled to her from Heaven... Pearl, although very spiritual, said that this had never happened before. The words started to come in to her mind, thick and fast, so she sat down and wrote what she was given. I know you will agree that this is so very beautiful and totally deserves a place in this book. Thank you Michael and Pearl for all that you do for the cat world, and for being a joy to know and work for.

Mollie the cat…

Mollie woke up to a beautiful May morning. She had a feeling in her tail that disaster was on its way. She started to wail, but instead of getting her usual hug, and some nice fish to eat, a harsh voice boomed at her to, 'Be quiet or you're in trouble.'

She went to her food bowl, it was hard and stale, and her water dish was empty, so feeling upset, she wandered into the garden. Whilst in the middle of a beautiful sleep in her favourite spot near a large flower bed, she was whisked up suddenly into a human's arms, pushed into a cat box and carried away to a place that was completely strange to her. She was then dumped in to some bushes and left there.

She lay there for a while, but then decided to explore. She was feeling lonely and frightened. She must find her way home to her loving human, but what if she could not find her way? She lay there wondering what was to become of her. She decided to wash herself, not forgetting her ears, as she was a very fastidious cat and liked to keep herself clean. The day was drawing to a close and it was getting a little chilly, and as she had not eaten all day she was feeling rather hungry and thirsty. She could not find any food but she found a small puddle and had a drink.

She decided to get a good sleep as she had to find a way of getting home tomorrow. Molly woke suddenly to an owl hooting. She looked up and saw an owl on a branch, as she had fallen asleep at the foot of a tree. She had heard hoots from owls before, and had seen them in the night when she loved to peep through the window. Mollie was a home loving cat and was not fond of roaming.

The next morning, Mollie woke to a fine day. Although she felt refreshed from her sleep, she was very hungry and thirsty, but what was there to eat? She wandered on and finally found a group of houses. At the final one, the people were very nice and gave her food and drink, and although not her favourite food, she was too hungry to worry about that. She stayed at that house for a while but thought she must carry on if she was to reach her home.

She continued walking for a long while, and the next house she came to she was not as lucky and was chased away. She carried on with her journey. Night came, so she found a spot to sleep. When she woke she felt very lonely and frightened, she was by now very hungry, and she decided that she would have to find her home soon, as things were getting desperate. She was not used to having to face the world on her own - she longed for her beautiful bed by the fireside, and her human to fuss her. She meowed forlornly to herself, and then started her long trek home, little knowing what lay ahead of her. She walked for most of the day. At one point she came across a stray dog, and he barked at her and gave chase. She managed to escape him but she felt weak and tired. Another time some naughty children threw stones at her but again she hid away from them.

Why was this happening to her she wondered? She used to love people and had always received love back, but she was beginning to feel a mistrust of them. As her journey continued she came across a small cat in a garden. He wanted to make friends and play, but Mollie, who was by now feeling very tired and exhausted, did not want to respond. Then a larger cat appeared and hissed and spat at her as this was his territory, so she ran away. Days turned in to nights, and still she carried on, but she was beginning to find it very hard as she had not eaten or had anything to drink for quite a while and was very weak. Sometimes she managed to find scraps dropped by people, but not very often.

The land seemed very bleak to Molly. Her coat was getting very matted where she hadn't the strength or will to clean herself. What was to become of her? What had happened to her loving human? What she did not know was, that they had died.

Molly was feeling ill now and weak from hunger, but she knew she must try to keep going if she wanted to reach her home. She searched desperately for food and water but there was little to be found. Sometimes on her journey she found someone who took pity on her, and gave her food and drink. Some humans she met were kind, some shooed her away and shouted at her, and she became very nervous and wary of people. The worst time for Mollie were the nights, they could be quite chilly, and her tummy being empty did not help. At night she always tried to find somewhere protective and out of sight to curl up and sleep.

By now Mollie was feeling frightened and she knew she was too ill to go much further. If she could not find a human to give her a home and love her, all hope was gone and something bad would happen to her. She knew that she had reached the time where she would either be found or she would sleep and wake no more. She found refuge under a bush, wrapped her tail around her, and tried to sleep. Then something wonderful happened...

A lady with her young son was out walking their dog, and on the way, the dog ran to the bush sniffing around, making an awful fuss. The lady was concerned in case he was worrying a small animal. She and her son peeped in to the bush and found Mollie. She gently lifted Mollie up, she was more dead than alive, but the lady wrapped her carefully in a jersey her young son had brought with him. They quickly got her home. They put Mollie carefully in to the ladies' car and took her straight to the vets. The surgeon and nurses were shocked at her condition, and gave her great care and all the treatment that was necessary. At last, after several weeks she was recovering well and went to a cat rescue.

Mollie knew she was being well looked after and had plenty of care and attention, but she had to sleep in a small cage. Although she was let out into the garden during the day with the other cats who were staying there, she preferred to be in her own box away from the others. What she really longed for was someone to find her and give her a home, and for her own fireside again, and for someone to love her. Once again, a little miracle happened for Mollie. She was dozing one afternoon when she woke at the presence of two people, a man and a woman. They started to stroke her and talk to her. She felt she liked these two people, and she thought that perhaps it might mean a new home for her. But after a while they went away and she was left feeling sad and disappointed. She curled up and went back to sleep. The next day about mid-day the two people came back and said they would like to give Mollie a home.

They brought that awful box with them, similar to the one that carried her out to the unknown, but she felt that this time it would be different. Although she did not like being shut in there, she was hopeful that it would not be for long. Sure enough they arrived home and let Mollie out of the box, but she was afraid and very nervous. After a good look round, she found a chair that slotted under the table in the kitchen and hid there.

Things were a little difficult for her and the humans for a while. Although she was fed well, looked after and loved, she had to get to know the humans, and they her. Soon there was a deep love and affection from Mollie, and given to Mollie. She is quite a cosseted cat as her humans give her as much as they can in many ways.

When she lost her eyesight her two humans were devastated, but she was content enough; she loved her home, her comfortable bed, and receiving all the love and attention she could possibly want from her humans. She would lie in her bed purring and washing herself, having a home once again.

One day her two loving humans knew that something was not right with her. She herself knew something was wrong as she was not feeling well. Her two humans took her to the vet's and she was taken in overnight, and put on a drip and given injections. All seemed well the next day, but after a while things were not right with Mollie; she found it hard to move around and her two humans were very upset for her. They took her back to the vet's and after examining her, they finally said there was nothing more they could do for Mollie, and a permanent sleep would be the right thing to do for her. Her two humans were devastated, and wept a great deal.

They took her dear little body home, kissed her, and wrapped her in her favourite blanket and buried her in a pretty spot in the garden. She has crocuses and small daffodils growing round her and her humans' favourite statue over her.

They both have wept many tears for their beautiful companion.

*****

Mike and Josie's cat Cardi

C – Caring and cute. **A** – Adorable and affectionate. **R** – Remembered fondly by all who knew him. **D** – Dominant but lovable. **I** – Intelligent and inquisitive.

What a name Cardi! Well with a full name of Wendbarry Cardinal, do you think we had any other choice but to call him Cardi?

We, myself Mike, and my wife Josie, remember the first time that we saw him in November 2001; he had been born on the 15th June that year, a skinny little thing with the biggest ears we've ever seen on a cat! On arriving home it wasn't long before he was dominating our Staffie dog called Zeus. Even when we bought them both new beds, Zeus ended up having to sleep in Cardi's smaller one! To say he was a dominant boy is an understatement, but who cared because he was extremely loving and loved by everyone who met him, cat lover or not. He was the most handsome Red Burmese you would ever see.

As a young cat he was inclined to explore, becoming a frequent, and welcome visitor to a retirement home nearby – they even provided him with his own water dish. Amazingly, he was allowed to go into the primary school, visiting as he wished, and to go into any classroom he chose. The kids loved him. One day, in he walked with a young tabby cat in tow. We had no idea who it belonged to and as time went by we named her Tabby (yes, very original) and decided that if she was going to stay with us she needed spaying. Sometime later Josie was sat in a neighbour's garden when Tabby walked in and we then discovered whose cat she was! They admitted that they were surprised to notice that she had been spayed but didn't make a fuss (how embarrassing). They moved house not long afterwards and left Tabby with us.

We moved temporarily and ended up living next door to a Methodist Preacher. He had no time for cats until Cardi arrived and as usual invited himself into the house. Before long he had Cardi sat on his lap whilst he prepared his sermons. We have no idea if Cardi provided divine inspiration.

On moving to our current home, both Cardi and Tabby soon settled well. Cardi thought that he had moved to the most magnificent food supermarket, with lots of rabbits, and even squirrels to chase and catch. Dear Tabby couldn't be bothered with this hunting malarkey, preferring to laze around in the large wooded garden.

The only trouble with Cardi's 'shopping' was that whatever he brought in was either alive or dead. Sometimes, he came in late at night with his 'gifts' even though we were in bed. We knew he had something because he always talked when climbing the stairs, but with a mouthful he couldn't do that. He found lots of places to hide them and sometimes a not very pleasant smell would become noticeable after a while. Despite this we always forgave him and loved him.

After a few years, Tabby became unwell and Cardi lovingly looked after her, rarely leaving her side until she passed. He knew that her time was up but did look a little lost when she went.

At 17 years old he appeared to be going strong but unfortunately, that was not the case. He started to lose weight and didn't want to eat. Despite all efforts of our wonderful vet and his staff, Cardi passed on the 5th August 2018, with his ashes being spread in a garden of remembrance.

We felt the loss terribly (especially Josie) and one of our fondest memories is that, as we drove into the drive (which a good 200ft from the house), he knew the sound of the car and always came to meet us, wanting to be carried on Josie's shoulder back to the house. How we miss that.

Fortunately enough, we had heard of a lady called Jackie Weaver, an Animal Psychic. Josie found her on Facebook and arranged a reading via Skype. This was the best thing we could have done, because she knew things about him that she had no way of knowing unless she was able to communicate with him. One of the things he said was that he was with two sisters who didn't look like him! We were thinking in cat terms, (as in cat siblings) but then we worked out that they are Kath and Shirley that he was talking about. They were Josie's younger sisters, both having passed with cancer. They both loved him very much when they were here with us, so we are happy that he is with them. Jackie described Cardi's personality, stating that he liked being in control, but also that he was very loving which was so correct. He really was a one off, and he knew it.

We were obviously very concerned as to whether we had done enough to help him. He communicated through Jackie that we were not to worry because he knew that it was his time to go, and didn't blame us for anything. He said that he would be with us forever, and for us not to worry about him because he is fine. This has enabled us to handle the bereavement better knowing that he was happy and at peace.

We have now re-homed a lovely two-year-old Blue Burmese called Desi; this was via the Burmese Cat Association. We were concerned that we had done this too early, but now we believe that it was fate that we have him. This was confirmed by Cardi, via Jackie, that he knew that we needed Desi and he made this happen. If anyone has any doubts about Jackie's ability, don't, she is one of the genuine ones. We found Jackie to be one of the most amazing, and kindest, people we have ever met.

*****

Claire and her dog Bronnie

I'm sure everyone believes their dog to be special, and their best friend, but Bronnie truly was my soul mate. She was a dog that everyone described as having a really soulful connection – it was almost as if she could look inside your soul, and really connect with you. I called her my angel in a fur coat.

You could say the internet found Bronnie for us. We already had a black and white collie X Lab called 'Pica' and we had been looking for a friend for her. Trawling through Facebook I suddenly thought I saw a photo of Pica! In fact, it was her look alike called 'Bronnie' on the 'Four paws' charity page. My excitement held no bounds – my gut feeling was telling me we had to go and see this look-a-like girl, Bronnie.

That Saturday we set up a meet and greet with her foster parents and our dog Pica. Funnily enough, as we stood outside their house knocking at the door, her foster dad came behind us and thought we had Bronnie with us there, and that she had somehow escaped! Her fosterers could not believe how alike the two of them were either. Bronnie was slightly smaller than Pica, although without a white tip on her tail, but otherwise they looked like sisters. After a short walk together, we arranged for Bronnie to come and stay on the Saturday with us. Following a lovely, and successful day, we adopted Bronnie and brought her to her forever home. We were told 'it was the fastest adoption in their history!'

In the early days it seemed as if Bronnie (soon to be Bron) was searching for someone. One day, we turned our back for a moment and she jumped down a 6 ft wall in our garden leaving us in a frantic search for her. I suddenly heard barking and looked down to see Bron stood there as if to say 'well come and get me as I can't get up by myself!' My husband, Lee, had to scale down our ladder and give Bron a fireman's lift back up to the garden. She jumped another high garden wall elsewhere and ran after someone walking up our nearby hillside. Once, out of the blue, she ran off in our park. It was very puzzling for us as the charity had checked her microchip etc and followed all the checks and procedures before re-homing her, so this discounted a loving dog just being simply lost.

Being a rescue, we had no idea of Bron's age, but it was estimated at approximately five to six-years-old. She was the gentlest and sweetest of dogs, quiet and liked her own space. Often, she would take herself off to a quiet area to snooze.

Bron & Pica had a good relationship and although they didn't lie together, they lived in happy companionship. Often photos taken of them left people puzzled as to whom was whom. This always delighted me for some strange reason! People always asked on meeting them if they were related or sisters; I liked to think so!

Bron became 'top dog' however, Pica liked to herd Bron when in the garden. Bron was an amazing ball catcher whilst Pica ran circles around her squeaking her own ball. It was always hysterical to watch, and when Bron had had enough, she'd take herself inside carrying her ball or watch the ball roll off and walk away herself.

She was a dog who knew her own mind! Bron put Pica in her place. One time when Pica attempted to take one of Bron's cuddly toys off her bed she growled at her. Bron didn't play with them but was not averse to letting anyone know they were hers and not to touch! She was also the most stubborn dog we had the pleasure of, if she didn't want to do anything or go anywhere, she would plonk herself down and you could not move her! Many a time we wrestled Bron onto the vet's scales, I'm sure she thought herself above such things!

As most labs are, Bron was a real foodie too. The moment she heard someone head to the kitchen, she would go running to join them. Her favourite place was to lie in front of the cooker just in case something happened to drop her way! She was not for moving from her ideal spot either!

She was a funny girl and had a habit often of walking backwards! She had her own method of coming downstairs to bed (we live in an upside-down house) and always went up two stairs at a time! She could show off when she wanted to! On work days before I left she would take herself back down to bed, like her mum. She too was not a morning person.

Ultimately, she was my shadow and my best friend. We did everything together: we got up together, went down to bed together, went from room to room together, walked in companionable silence in the park side-by-side.

Bronnie loved to sit outside with me just relaxing, and sniffing the air. This she loved to do most of all! She also loved cuddles and would often lay her head on my knee or a paw on my arm and gave the best kisses.

Gradually she slowed down. In the early years she suffered with elbow callouses which she always tolcratcd with me fussing over and trying out different treatments. She really was a dog who coped with anything, such was her gentle nature. She started to have various degrees of tummy troubles and when we started investigations, it was discovered she had some liver and kidney damage. Various medications worked and others didn't, but we tried all that was available. Eventually, in latter weeks, we decided her quality of life mattered more. Especially when it came to food, as the awful kidney food that we were asking her to eat, was obviously being eaten out of hunger, not with enjoyment. So Bron delighted in us cooking fabulous and tasty food just for her. She had: heart, liver, kidneys, bowls of sausages, you name it. The stink was horrendous!

On two occasions we thought we had lost her. One time Lee carried her into the vets after her legs had given way on her only for her to walk back out of the surgery! The vet and staff were amazed, and amused. We luckily had a very caring vet whom Bronnie really liked. The vet called her 'The comeback kid!', and she definitely was! This was a dog with more than one life, and I was thankful on these occasions that she was so stubborn. I even went as far to think she was getting a bit better as she was still enjoying her walks in the park. We arranged a professional doggy photo shoot at home – she was not really amused by that but we got some very cherished pictures out of it. She even enjoyed a holiday with us as we rented a Dogs Trust cottage in Cornwall. Our girl truly was a fighter!!

However, the vet told us when 'it' happened, it would be fast but I was not prepared as to how fast. People ask, 'how do you know when the time is right' but you do! She looked at us very mournfully, and we both saw in her eyes that she'd finally had enough of fighting this awful illness. Her body was filling up with toxins and they were obviously affecting her. She was having toilet accidents and we knew that distressed her – even when so poorly she would always nudge us, whether night or day, to let us know she needed a loo break. She was not wanting to eat or drink, albeit her last food was Aunt Bessie's mash eaten off a spoon. Truly, a dog after her mum's own heart.

We had previously arranged for Bron's vet to come out to us on the Monday and administer the final act of kindness at home in her bed. We knew by the Sunday morning we could not let her go on any longer, although we were reluctant to use out of hours service as we had only lost Pica four months earlier to a very sudden illness. However, we both knew we could not see her suffer and that it must be our final act of kindness.

Bronnie lost her 'Earthly suit' as I like to think of it on June 9th 2019. On that day I lost my 'bestie' and my 'soul mate.' I would constantly whisper those words in her ear and I think she knew what they meant. A part of my heart and soul went with Bron, whilst she left a part of hers with me. To lose one dog is horrendous, but to lose two in less than six months was downright cruel. I knew I needed confirmation that she was safe and well, and that we hadn't waited too long to release her. There was only one person for me to turn to and that was Jackie Weaver. I had read all of Jackie's books, which gave me comfort and, in a way felt right, as my maiden name was Weaver too.

The date was set for July 20th at 12pm via Skype webcam. I knew I had made the right decision as immediately I felt at ease speaking with Jackie. Jackie described Bronnie as a 'gentle girl, wouldn't hurt or harm a fly', so I knew straight away my girl was with us. She was gentle and even on occasions when she met dogs who continually bothered her, she wouldn't tell them off. Bron said how she had a huge loving heart and was gracious with other dogs but happy by herself.

A picture of Bron resting her head on my knee was given with me calling her 'mummy's girl'. Such accuracy and clarity of our life together.

Jackie talked about Bron being a dog who could look into your soul, which couldn't have been truer! Bron even told Jackie what I always said about our relationship... it was that I felt like I'd known her all my life! Bron even said, 'how blessed we were to have each other'. I knew my girl was right there with me at that moment as I experienced 'chills' as if she was right beside me. This happened a few times during the reading. It was the strangest, and amazing sensation. Jackie explained they can do that with their energy to really validate their presence.

Bron remembered how she enjoyed spending gentle time with me. Even if it was just our routine which we did, late night cuddles, her paw laid on my arm or her head on my knee – such a special and close time together. I knew Bron had been reading my mind when talking about me, she said, 'You never knew you could love that much' and that I had never loved a dog as I had loved her. I couldn't have described our relationship any better.

I constantly would smoother her head with kisses. She told me to keep on imagining doing as she could receive them up into her spirit energy. She knew I still said 'goodnight Bronnie' and 'good morning

Bronnie'. That is something I will continue to do, each and every day.

We may have received the answer as to why Bron seemed to be doing her random searching when we first had her. When Jackie told us she felt she may have come from a broken home as the people had separated or couldn't, for whatever reason, keep her. This made sense because we always felt that she hadn't been abused and had been loved. So, at first, she may have been thinking they were still out there for her. I am glad that she then turned her love and attention to us and never looked back.

I felt more at ease when Bron said she'd never really suffered in her life and, as regards to her passing, she acknowledged that we had got it absolutely right and how we just 'knew'. When she stopped eating we knew she had had enough, but was keen to let me know that it was just how things go. She remembered having a scan and how the last six days she really wasn't herself, having gone downhill so fast. The illness had taken her over.

Jackie said she was with my grandfather; he had come through many times in previous clairvoyant readings! I asked if she had made contact with our other dog, Pica. We felt she had grieved at Pica's passing, refusing to eat for days. Jackie said that she would join up with everyone bit by bit and, to remember that she hadn't been in spirit for long.

Strangely, Bron even described the cremation box we received back and how on the top, a small posy of artificial flowers had been placed. It makes it all the more special knowing that she can see it too.

Being able to talk to my girl, and receive confirmation that she was indeed happy and well, provided me with the reassurance I had been looking for. I know, just as in life, she is still with me wherever I go, even on those trips to the bathroom! I feel able to ask Bron for guidance, especially when Jackie told me how attentive she was to me, when with me here on Earth.

Significantly butterflies became a sign to me after Jackie told me to watch out for them. On three different occasions whilst out walking our other dog, I asked Bron to show me a sign that she was walking with me. On each occasion a minute or so after, a butterfly would appear either in front of me, or to the side. I knew she was there! That has provided great comfort to me.

Our happy girl I know is very much alive and just waiting for me. I try not to be sad as I know one day, we will all be back together again and when that happens, I'm sure my grandfather will bring her to me running and wagging her tail as she always did.

I am so glad I had this reading with Jackie when my world crumbled. She has restored my faith that we are all destined to be back together again one day. I feel that I am honouring Bron's memory in writing this. Bron showed me the incredible capacity of dogs to love and trust, and she has indeed made me the person I am today. I know we had, and still have, an incredibly special and unique relationship. I'm pretty certain I will speak to Bronnie and hopefully, Pica, again through Jackie, if only to know how they are doing and if they've met up. However, for now, I know my girl is watching over and guiding me. I will keep asking, and talking, to her as I know she will be listening to me.

*****

I totally understand the pain of that 'decision'. So, in every book, I have included this poem given to me, straight from spirit to help ease peoples' pain.

Letting Go

Your heart is bursting, searing with pain
That physical touch never to be had again
You only let them go because you so clearly care
They might not be here but they are surely up there.
You feel the pull and the tear of your heart
You feel torn inside and ripped apart
The enormity of choosing what best to do
It was done with your love, as they looked to you.
We don't enter into this without thought or care
We do it because the compassion is there
The choice to stop pain and distress of the one we love
Can only be guided by you and the angels above.
Many spirits have come through and given me their word
Your tears of sorrow and distress they heard
But they are free and happy and hold no ill will
Whatever was wrong could not have been cured with a pill.
The height of pain is a measuring device
It shows how deeply you felt throughout their life
With your love given for this most selfless act
They at least left this earth with their heart intact.
Now up yonder and free to roam

This is another level, like a new home
The day will come when you go up there too
They're ready and waiting to meet and embrace you.
If you truly did this from your genuine heart
You were so brave and helped them depart
Your love and courage was seen from above
This really was your strongest act of love.
If you could ask them now, what might they say?
"In my life, that was actually only one single day,
Please remember the rest, the joy, love and play,
For I look down from above and remember it that way."
As time has passed you may at last feel some ease
Maybe a pet has come for you to please
Animals are not selfish and want you to share
They left that space for another needing your love and care.
We are truly honoured to share in their space
Think back and let that smile adorn your face
The precious time you had could never be measured
Your lasting memories are of those you truly treasured.

Jackie Weaver 2009

*****

Erica and her cat Bear

Bear came into our lives three weeks after I lost my beautiful cat Benny. I had never had my own cat and Benny was my absolute soulmate and I was inconsolable.

So, I was quite shocked when my husband Adam suggested we go to London's Battersea cat and dog home after just three weeks – What was he thinking?

Despite that, we went and had a look at the dogs and did consider one, but it was just not the right time for a dog. So, as we were there anyway, we decided to only have a look at the cats.

My heart was so heavy with Benny's loss but would it be so wrong to give a home to another cat who so needed one? I wouldn't be replacing Benny, but could I find room in my heart to adopt another?

After several attempts at befriending some cats, I had nearly given up until one of the girl carers suggested we meet Burgess. My husband wanted a big cat, and Burgess was a big boy. We were told, 'Burgess is a beautiful big boy, loves a cuddle but he does have a bit of a history'.

Adam likes to tell the story of how Burgess's cubicle was in a dark, dusty corner and how this long forgotten big black beauty prowled out to see what humans had been brought before him this time.

It wasn't like that at all! Although he did prowl down, yawning, looking slightly put out that he had been disturbed as the carer was reading his history: He had been an unneutered and un-microchipped stray for at least six months and apparently, he had attacked the woman who had tried to take him in, but then he had attacked her cats too. Reluctantly, she had taken him to Battersea. All the time that she was reading out the history of this supposedly vicious cat, Burgess was lying on his back with his legs in the air and I was stroking his belly and playing with him. Here was an absolute beauty looking for love and a home. Vicious? Not a bit – this boy was coming home with us.

When we got home, he crept out of his basket and promptly sat on Adam's chair and that is how it was from then on. We renamed him Brewster Bear, always to be known as Bear. Where Bear sat, that was his seat! He was like the eponymous cat that got the cream ... King of the Castle. Bear had found his forever home!

I learnt that grieving for Benny and learning to love Bear were two very separate emotions. Bear just sat with me, or on me, for hours, and within a few short weeks, Bear had stolen our hearts.

He was funny, gentle, loving, stubborn and naughty. He was extremely OCD, a cat that required habit and order, and we pandered to it all. He could wrap us round his little paw. Bear literally healed my heart. He would hold out his paw and just gently rest it on my face or stroke my face. He was just pure unadulterated joy – he was playful and would bound everywhere, full of energy and life. He was pure loving energy.

Bear loved Adam and Adam adored Bear, but he was definitely mine. If I was out, he would sit on Adam's lap quite happily but as soon as I came home he would jump off Adam and onto me. He would lie with Adam in the morning and as soon as I stirred, he would be cuddled up with me. Luckily Adam was not offended; he could see how happy Bear made me.

Bear would jump up onto the table, knowing that he was not allowed to, so I would pick him up before he got told off. Bear would cling onto me like a baby – he knew he would get a huge cuddle and he did. He absolutely knew how to play us both and he made us laugh.

After just four glorious years of pure joy and happiness, early one morning Adam found our beautiful Bear dead downstairs. He was like he had just keeled over. It was sudden and probably instant. The shock we both felt was overwhelming. We were both literally heartbroken.

Jackie had done an amazing reading for me when I lost Benny and I went to her again for a reading with Bear. The reading was all I hoped it would be… and more. The accuracy was staggering.

She knew his character exactly and used phrases that we would use to describe him. Jackie used the words 'I was a proper cat'. That was exactly what Adam would say about him. 'Bear is a proper cat – a big boy with bags of personality'. Also, 'I was a loving big boy' which he absolutely was.

She described Bear as a 'chirpy, happy soul with no angst about him at all and a real bruiser but not aggressive'. That was Bear all over. He was so chilled out! As Jackie related, 'He enjoyed a quiet life but was also full of fun'.

Bear knew that we worried about him straying and getting lost due to his history before he came to us, but he explained that when he got to us, he knew he was home and was not going to lose us now. He no longer wandered; he stayed safe and close by. It was a complete relief to us that he made it home before he passed so suddenly. Of Bear's transition, in typical fashion of a chilled out cat, Bear reported that it was 'nothing drastic'. It was drastic to us but to him... not a bit!

During the reading, Jackie said that Bear was always with me and to prove it to me, Bear had shown to her a page of writing in a diary or workbook and the writing was on a slant – not written on a straight line. I pondered for a moment and I flicked through my diary I had used that morning and I was amazed, as I had written down a list of clients I had seen … on a slant rather than straight list. Bear could see everything and I believe absolutely that he is with me. That was so specific.

Jackie also mentioned that Bear had shown her how my previous cat Benny used to jump up to drink water from something. I couldn't think at the time what that meant, but later realised that Benny used to jump up to drink out of an ornamental bird bath, and incredibly, one of the first things Bear did when he went out, was to drink out of the bird bath in exactly the same way. I now believe Bear was showing me what he knew Benny used to do. (I found an old photo and emailed it to Jackie. She was very appreciative and said that it explained her vision. She said it is so lovely to get validation of things that people cannot remember at the time as it proves, the only one to tell her must have been the pet she was talking to.)

When I said how sad I was that we only had Bear for four years, he said, 'Could you imagine me getting old?' In truth, No. Bear either bounded everywhere, full of energy and fun or he lay down and chilled. There was not a lot in between. Bear was not one to get old and infirm and he would have hated it.

The accuracy of the reading was amazingly comforting. Jackie relayed information to me that was so specific. There was nothing that I didn't get.

The parting shot from my Bear was about two cats that I was dithering about getting. We had been offered a chance to re-home two cats. I had not mentioned this to Jackie at all, but she brought up the possibility of re homing 'twins'? They are not twins but had been brought up together. I wondered about the term 'twins'... and a couple of weeks later, I was going to see them, and Adam asked me how the twins were? It was completely unprompted! Bear was encouraging in my decision to get them, and knew of my desire to nurture but I was unsure due to my sadness.

A few weeks on, and after much deliberation, we now have 'the twins'. A boy and girl, age 9 and 10. Their names Benny and Bea – we have not changed their names at all, incredibly that is what they were called! You could not make it up and Adam always refers to them as the twins!

Bear was more of a joy than I could ever have imagined. He too was my soul-mate... part of my very being. The heartbreak I felt was all consuming, and still is as I write this. I miss him every minute of every day, but due to my reading with Jackie, I absolutely know he is here with me. I have had numerous signs from him and the reading is part of that proof that Bear is with me and watches over me.

*****

Victoria and her Dog Ruby

It started back twelve years ago. I wanted to get a little dog who would love to be cuddled, follow me around, and for me to love and care for him or her. I started looking at different breeds, and decided I wanted a King Charles Cavalier. I found a breeder in the South of England and was happy to travel there as, although the puppies were not even born, the lady was Kennel Club registered and seemed very knowledgeable. For some reason, although I really wanted a puppy soon, I decided to wait.

When I finally got the call to say the puppies were born, I was told there were five girls to choose from. My heart sunk as I originally wanted a boy but, as I had waited this long, I decided to go and see these little girls anyway. As I entered into the room with the puppies, a little five-week-old ruby coloured puppy came running towards me... it was love at first sight! My little Ruby, as I chose to call her, was meant for me.

I was living with my parents at the time and had to wait until she was nine weeks old for us to go and collect her. When the time came, to say I was excited was an understatement. When we arrived back home and took her in to the house, my little Ruby ran straight to her new bed, and jumped in! Ruby was home she never looked back. We all loved her and treated her like a baby. We took turns playing with her and she always shared herself amongst us all.

She made friends with this lovely black Labrador dog called Jack; she would get so excited to see him. It was sweet to watch as Jack spotted her, sat down and when she got close he would then bound up towards her, complete with a sniff and a lick. His owner always had little treats, and would bend down to give her a treat too. He always commented how lovely and sweet she was.

Over the next five years we did everything together: She came to barbeques, parties and of course long walks to so many different places. We would regularly have family get-togethers where she would always be running around giving affection to all the family and friends.

Thinking back now, I knew that she was so happy as my mum said one day, that she was not sure who loved who more, me her or her me. To me, she was like my real baby, like I had given birth to her. I think that's why I was finding it so hard to let her go.

When she was six years old, I met the man of my dreams and when we got married, we became a complete family. Before we got married, we had a free photo shoot as part of our wedding package. The photographer decided to do the pictures at our local park, complete with Ruby. It was an amazing day and we had pictures of the three of us and ones of Ruby running about. I had no idea at the time how very precious these pictures would be.

Married life was wonderful and the three of us would go everywhere together – new places to walk and see, and evenings down at the coast. Ruby loved every minute, especially being in the car; it was her favourite. We even took her fishing a couple of times. We would camp out near the lake and cook food. Ruby was in her element with all the smells, the fresh air and simply being with her 'mummy and daddy'.

When Ruby reached nine-years-old, I noticed she was less interested in walking so took her to the vets. She had blood tests, an ultrasound (or 'sonogram' as I later found out it was also called) and heart tests. It showed she had an enlarged heart and one leaky heart valve but fortunately, with right medication, she was happy and loving life once again and for the next two years, she was fine.

By then, we had moved house and were more in the countryside. Ruby had a larger garden and there were horses to watch just metres away. She also had two new doggy friends belonging to the neighbours either side of us. Ruby loved it there. She would sunbathe in the garden and talk to her dog neighbour Tia, who was also a Cavalier. The other side was Harry, a lovely Golden Retriever, and they would give each other kisses, and he would follow her around.

Sadly, later on that year, we had vet visits pretty much every week to check her heart and salt levels. By now, one of the tablets was a very high dose so the vet suggested another type of tablet. It really, really helped and every time we took her to the vets, he would say to her, 'Hello Ruby dog – you are a little miracle.' And to us, 'Whatever you are doing, carry on doing it.' We did: I would massage her joints and take her for little walks and then long rides in the car. She would put her head close to the open window and look out having the fresh air sweep over her face.

One weekend we went to Poo Sticks Bridge in Hartfield (East Sussex), which was the Winnie the Pooh bridge in the books with Christopher Robin. It was a lovely sunny evening, a sweet and memorable day for us. Sadly, not long after that, we had an emergency visit to the vets as her tummy became swollen with fluid. It was decided they would have to use a syringe to drain the fluid off and try another medication. With that done, I took her home and watched her all night. The next morning she was bright, happy and running around; it was the best feeling.

When we had the follow up the vet advised us that the new medication was only a short-term remedy to give her a better quality of life, but it would not last. We walked out of there and, amazingly, had another six weeks of fun. We took her to down to the coast – it was a bright sunny day. Ruby had so much life in her running around and smelling the sea air. I now know that was going to be her last big day out.

It was not long before Ruby was finding it hard to walk and not really wanting to eat. She was having difficulty with her breathing and another drain of her tummy fluid done. The next day my little Ruby wasn't right, restless and looked at me differently; she was so tired and unhappy and we decided it was too much for her. Her little body was struggling and her quality of life was so reduced, so my little Ruby when to sleep on 16th October 2017.

Writing this now takes me right back to that afternoon… I wrapped her up in her little blanket, complete with her little bear. I told her she was the best thing that ever happened to me and that we can meet up in my dreams, and still go to places together.

I came home knowing my world had changed… Dark lonely days followed. I had a broken heart and was crying all the time. I missed my Ruby; life seemed grey. All I seemed to want to do was go to the places we taken her to as somehow it made me feel closer to her. I was feeling all emotions especially guilt, 'Should I have waited another day – was it too soon?' I needed to look for some help and up came Jackie Weaver on the Internet. I was drawn to her so I looked at her website, and read the reviews. I decided to go ahead as I had to speak to my Ruby again. I needed to know she was okay as I had worried, and cared for Ruby for twelve years, so how do you tell your heart to stop worrying? So I emailed Jackie and couldn't wait for the day.

From the start, Jackie made me feel relaxed and said she had asked Ruby to tell her about herself. Ruby had told her that she was a dear sweet girl who looked good all the time, and when I asked her to come up on the sofa for cuddles, she would straight away. She showed a 24 hour clock to Jackie saying she was checked all the time. This was so true as we had a rota to keep an eye on her. Ruby talked about long rides in the car which she loved and just watched the scenery go by. I said when she was older we would just take her for a car ride, as she loved it. Jackie said that she thought that was so sweet and thoughtful of us.

Jackie said that she felt it was only the last couple of years that Ruby had been ill. I agreed. Ruby then went on to say how she had a 'sonogram' and that her heart was failing and sadly, the result wasn't surprising. Jackie said that the word 'sonogram' was different and one she did not use. At that point, she quickly 'Googled' it and amazingly, it is an alternative word for an ultrasound! It made us both smile and wonder at the extent of spirit knowledge – amazing, if you ask me! Jackie said how Ruby was thirsty all the time, which was so true. When Ruby was put on to the new tablets, she would go through two bowls of water a day.

Ruby said that we had done the right thing to let her go and it was done out of love. She said she was brave throughout all her heart issues, and yes, she so was. At this point, I had tears running down my face as Ruby said, 'Don't think of me when I was ill, think when I was happy running around, that is how I am. I am now crystal and free and that we would see each other again.' She said a man called Brian was now spoiling her. I can't place him although Jackie says sometimes the name will come to light later and I am glad she is being spoilt by someone.

Ruby was showing Jackie a black and tan boy Cavalier, so maybe a new dog? This was really funny as, my husband and I had been thinking of getting another one around a year ago, and it was exactly that! After a lot of consideration, we decided Ruby may not have liked having a little puppy bounding around, being of senior years herself. I did explain this to Jackie and Ruby yet again, showed her the same picture and seemed like she was excited about it. Jackie said, 'Never say never, and that every animal that is to come to you, will. Just like Ruby did.'

Our conversation was sad, lovely and warm. It made me feel my little Ruby was around me still. Other things Jackie had told me were so true. She said that Ruby was looking over me and when I found Ruby's little winter coats, I folded them up and put them away. That was exactly what I had done. I had packed everything in a keepsake box with all of Ruby's things.

I will miss my little Ruby forever but I'll always remember our conversation with love in my heart. Thank you Jackie for making me feel connected to my Ruby again – you have a lovely gift.

'I love and miss you my little spirit Ruby. Watch over me from time to time and I know that this isn't goodbye forever, just bye for now. See you over the rainbow.' xxxxx

*****

Michael and Pearl's cat Lucy

Lucy was a pretty little thing and we were totally unable to resist her.

We were at a cattery seeking a new companion having lost two beautiful cats within three days – one to mouth cancer, the other had had a seizure. Being heart-broken was an understatement. At the time we thought we could not face the sadness of departure again, and had decided not to have another cat.

The emptiness of the house told us otherwise, so here we were at a rescue centre seeking to adopt two cats, preferably elderly ones, so that we could give them a comfortable and loving home. As we passed the windows, we saw a number of the cats who were very young (too young for us), and some of the older cats who stayed at the back of their pens and did not respond to us. It was a rather sad experience to see these little creatures so clearly out of their known environment. We came to the next window and a very pretty little cat came up to us and started talking to us. She was rubbing the side of her head against the window and was such a pretty little thing. We opened her pen and she was so happy to be fussed and cuddled, it was an immediate decision.

Her name was Lucy and she was fourteen years old. Her owner, after fourteen years, had taken her to the cattery claiming that she had become allergic to her. (Seemed odd, but who were we to question?) We asked to adopt Lucy and explained that we would also like a second cat to adopt. However, we were told that Lucy had to be the only cat in the household, so we dismissed the idea of another as this girl seemed to want to be with us and we wanted her. The young lady who was showing us around seemed very pleased when we agreed to take Lucy saying, "I did not want her to die here." This we assumed was because Lucy was elderly and had been in the cattery for five months with no one taking an interest in her.

When we collected Lucy, we were told she was on a special diet and we were given an overwhelming amount of food to take away. Except for being informed about her diet, there was no mention of Lucy's health and if there had been, it would not have mattered as we were adopting Lucy for better or worse. As we were departing, a young lady came to us and said, 'The vet thinks she could live for a couple of years' but then someone in the background commented, 'or a couple of weeks.' This we did not understand and, although a little surprised by it, we just wanted to get Lucy home to start giving her the love we were sure she deserved.

She truly was an absolute joy. Lucy had very short legs, white paws and was white around her mouth and chest; she really was such a pretty little thing. It was fun to watch her with her little short legs scramble onto the coffee table and across our settee so that she could sit on our laps to be fussed and cuddled.

Lucy settled in and we were all very happy but, after five weeks she started to act a little differently; instead of coming to us for a cuddle, she would settle on the rear doormat, which seemed odd. I mentioned this to our vet who suggested it might be cooler there, which might suggest that she was perhaps running a temperature? Lucy was taken straight to the vets for a full check up and yes, she had got a temperature, so they kept her in for tests. That evening we received a phone call telling us that Little Lucy had peritonitis (inflammation of a lining in the stomach area), which is a critical condition needing prompt treatment. The vet explained they would need to drain her stomach of the infection and if we were agreeable, this would be done the following morning.

On the way to work I pass the vets so the next morning I called in to see how Lucy was. I opened the door to her pen and stroked her gently, but she did not respond. I thought that she was just too tired after her treatment, so gave her a kiss, and went on my way. Shortly after my visit, I received a phone call to let me know that dear little Lucy had passed away in her sleep.

We were heartbroken, but also really angry that an owner of fourteen years who must have known that she was sick, plus also the cattery, (complete with their own vet) who had her for five months, had not attempted to give her all the help she needed. The conversation "The vets says…" came back to our minds but had we been advised of the truth, we would still have adopted her, but instead taken her straight to our vet for help and advice.

Lucy was cremated, then once again, we turned to Jackie Weaver for help and comfort. Through Jackie, we learned that Lucy had been pleased to go, that she was no longer in pain, and that she was happy. She was so very grateful to us for giving her love and comfort at the end of her life, and to have left the rescue centre. She also pointed out that at least we noticed something was wrong and took her to the vets straightaway, so her suffering was lessened. She told us that she had been a loving cat to her previous owner – how sad that they gave up such a sweet girl who had given them so much. As hard as this had been, we let her know that although we had only had her for a short time; she had given us so much joy and had helped us cope with the loss of our other two cats. Interestingly, Jackie said she heard the name 'Billy'. We said we did not know a Billy, but she said to bear this in mind as it could perhaps relate to a future cat. Amazingly it did, and in an unusual way!

As always, we decided that we could not face losing any more cats, however, the emptiness of the house saw us back at another cattery, a different one needless to say. A young man escorted us around the area that contained cats for rehoming. Once again, we explained that we were looking for a mature cat and, as we walked past the pens, there was one that was draped in sheets. We asked the reason for this and were told it was because the cat behind the blinds was very anti social. By covering the cage over, the blinds stopped the cat being bothered by people passing by and other cats in their pens. As this was being explained, a longhaired tabby cat appeared from behind the blinds and came over to us. The young man was surprised, but this cat was not looking threatening in any way. Obligingly, the lad opened the door for us, and this so-called anti-social cat started to lick and kiss our hands with great enthusiasm!

We were sold immediately. The long-haired tabby was a nine-year-old female who had been in the cattery for a month. She had been refusing to have anything to do with anyone, and when he told us her name, you could have knocked us over with a feather, as she was called BILLIE!

This now leaves two questions… 1. How could Lucy know that we would adopt a cat called Billie? 2. Why did Billie behave so anti socially until we appeared? She is gentle and loving, and we simply adore her. Jackie says that it was all meant to be, and that all animals that are supposed to come to us, will! Billie is very beautiful, but her anti-social behaviour stopped people from adopting her so that she was still there ready for us.

One of the first things we did was take her to the vet for an M.O.T and she passed with flying colours. Phew! Thank you for coming into our life Billie. We adore you and look forward to you spending the rest of your life with us. We know you were Heaven sent, and how clever Lucy was to have told us about you before we ever knew you. Thank you Lucy, and as sad as we were to lose you so very quickly, you have helped guide us to another needing love, and of that, we have got so much to give.

*****

Alison and her Horse Cree

Cree was my beautiful Appaloosa mare of nearly 20 years. She was the light of my life and I loved her more than anything in the world. When we were younger we competed in show jumping and later in life she pulled a trap (horse carriage) for me.

Cree was very gentle and sensitive but very forward going and giddy! She liked to jog everywhere and I learned over the years not to argue with her and to just sit quiet and basically let her do what she wanted. She loved the trap as she could jog really fast and extend at her pleasure like a perfect 'road horse'. She was very clever and I was so tuned into her. We had a beautiful bond that was apparent to everyone who knew us. She was like my other half.

In 20 years my life wasn't all plain sailing and through bad times, both emotional and financial, Cree was my rock and the sunshine of my every day. In May of 2012 when she was 19 years old she went down with awful laminitis in both her front feet. (Laminitis is a condition that affects their feet and is desperately painful.) I was devastated as she'd always been so fit and healthy. Having spent five and a half months in the stable, she literally shrunk having lost her muscle and condition. I had to limit her food/grass etc. as condition is often triggered that way. It was a stressful and painful time for her however, my vet and farrier said they were sure she'd pull through and recover.

There were times when I thought I was losing her. On Christmas Day of that year, we rode for the first time. It was an amazing day; I was honestly euphoric. Over the next two years I was managing to keep her comfortable while maintaining a full quality of life. She was never completely sound (horse term for not lame), but we rode most of the time bar a few times when she had a set back, or 'wobble' as I referred to it. Following the summer of 2013, the walls of her feet were literally non-existent due to pulling off her heart-bar shoes (special shaped remedial shoes) whilst in the field throughout the summer. We decided to take her shoes off. She did the whole winter 'barefoot' in the stable, and had hoof boots on in the field and for exercise. She actually remained 'sound' all winter and we were out every day, jig jogging along of course, with me sweating and exhausted by the time we got back to the yard, but not Cree – she was incredible.

The following summer of 2014 she seemed to 'wobble' more and more consistently and I was struggling to keep her sound enough to ride. The time before last she went lame it turned out to be an abscess in her foot. I felt, for the first time, she was sore in her back – this can happen I know as they try and hold their weight back off their front feet. She enjoyed a massage and seemed to recover before the next set back, which this time she was apparently now lame in her back end. I did the usual thing and gave her pain relief and tried to nurse her through it. She was still going out in the field for around four hours a day, however she just wasn't improving – it was difficult for me to see her so crippled and struggling like that. At this point I decided to have her x-rayed just to see exactly what was going on inside her feet, as it all had to be connected to her condition.

On Friday morning of the 3rd October 2014 my vet arrived followed by my farrier who'd been amazing throughout and became my therapist! When I saw the x-rays I was shocked. The bones had rotated and the tips where almost touching the sole of her foot. I knew myself it didn't look good – my farrier's face said it all. My vet was talking about more specialist shoeing and treatment for the bones to re-align but it would be at least 18 months for this to happen, if ever. Everything in me wanted to say, 'Yes let's try that,' but 'I think I should have her put to sleep,' came out of my mouth. I was shocked and stunned in that split second that I'd said it. I think it was my instinct talking above my heart and brain. My vet and farrier instantly agreed and said it was time and that I was doing the right thing by her. It was all so surreal; I couldn't believe I was going along with it. It was the most painful thing I'd ever had to do. I was both shocked and devastated.

The following days and weeks were extremely difficult; I felt like my whole world was gone. I was struggling most of all with the torment and torture of having moments of feeling like, had I done it too soon? Could she have coped? Maybe she wasn't ready? Everybody, including my non-horsey friends, were adamant I did the right thing, at the right time. I knew logically that, had I left it, she wasn't going to get any better and her end could have been horrendous and horrible for us both. I have to say, she left with her dignity as the day before she had been out enjoying time with her friends in the paddock and, on that fateful day, it was sunny with a lovely fresh breeze for her. However, I was still torturing myself and no matter what anyone said, or how much I tried to have a word with myself, I needed to hear it from Cree.

I searched the Internet and found Jackie. I waited for the phone call. At first Cree was explaining what kind of horse she was, gentle, reliable, and safe and we'd been on different yards over the years and she took it all in her stride. Very true. She presented a picture of x-rays to Jackie and said she'd been walking on the outsides of her feet. She had also been sore in her backend and she'd been worried about the mud in winter and didn't feel she could cope with slipping. This made sense as my whole town is one big hill so our land, and the winter field, is mostly on a gradient. She went on to say she'd been a fun horse and been 'unstoppable!' Yes, how very true Cree!

She showed us a portrait of herself and at the time I was being quite coy about what I was saying. I am a portrait painter and I'd painted her at the time when she was really ill. I hadn't painted for many years but I had to do it at the time as I thought I may have been losing her. I found it very therapeutic at the time and ended up painting more portraits for my friends. To cut a long story short, within six months somehow I had a pet portrait website up and running and also another of canvas contemporary paintings too! Both of which were already reasonably successful and I was already by then working as a semi-professional artist. Cree brought the portrait up again later in the conversation and explained that she inspired me, which she did, and that she was still with me when I was painting and she was helping me! Bless her. She also told me I am under-charging and told Jackie I'm magnificent and I should believe in myself more! Bless you Cree.

She also explained that she hadn't been in pain but she was uncomfortable. She knew I'd been disappointed and sad every time she'd gone lame. She told me not to feel guilty and she knew I'd done everything I could for her. She said there was nothing anybody could have done and was showing Jackie the undersides of her front feet. She said in the end I could see it in her face that she was now really struggling and that she's not hurt or angry with me and she knows how tough it has been for me. This was the part of the conversation I needed to hear. I also beat myself up as she'd been a little chubby when she went down with the Laminitis, however, turned out she had another condition called Cushing's disease. There were no visible signs of it at all but a side effect can be the on-set of Laminitis. Cree explained very specifically that it was nothing to do with the weight; it was all to do with the Cushing's disease and that I'm not to beat myself up about that either. That's me told!

She then went on to tell Jackie she wasn't frightened of anything and we had fun and again described herself as 'very keen'. At this point, I was both laughing and crying at the same time. She said we were totally suited and that even though my life had changed dramatically over the years, both emotionally and financially at times, I'd never turned my back on her; she was my priority whatever. She also said she'd never 'gone miserable' on me throughout her illness and pain. Very true; she never changed at all until that last couple of weeks she did look sad and tired, but she was never grouchy.

Cree commented that the photo I had sent to Jackie was rather unique. It was of her head but taken from behind her as she was looking out of her stable. This made it from dark to light and it's quite dramatic how the light hits her face and highlights her features. She told me she'd like me to paint this one as I've been thinking of painting her again, which is also true!

I am at present selling my house and planning on relocating from Manchester to the Lincolnshire coast. I'm doing this alone and leaving all my friends and a business of 20 years behind in search of a better life. I wanted a much nicer place to be and hope to be working full time as a professional artist, albeit very scary! I asked Jackie to ask Cree about my future plans. Cree said I was going it alone but, 'you won't be on your own' and I'm looking for peace and quiet. She then volunteered I needed to get my 'braveometer' out. How funny! Cree was so brave everywhere we went and all that we did together. Even throughout her illness, she was incredible. I'm totally inspired by her and feel an inner strength from her gained through my communication with Jackie. I have absolutely no doubts Cree will be coming with me and enjoying the beach with me again – we loved going to the beach when we were both young and fit!

As I write this, it is three months since I lost her and I'm still having awful moments of grave sadness. I've been crying my eyes out while writing this however, now when I feel myself lulling into self-torture, I think of my chat with her and Jackie. Fortunately, I wrote it all down in pointers so I remember the whole conversation; it instantly soothes and reassures me and lightens the pain. She was an amazing mare and I'm honoured she was mine. I'm thankful for all she gave me and taught me too. I know she will be with me, guiding me wherever I end up living and in whatever I am doing.

*****

Ciara and her cat Ginger

Ginger, otherwise known as "Ginge" was a beautiful, male, marbled Ginger cat. He was ginger all over except for white at the tip of his tail, under his chin and a spot on his belly. I used to call him daft however he was anything but. I wish I knew what age he was, but as I found him – or he found me rather, I could only hazard that he was coming on seven years old when I lost him. He was a person in a cat body. He had his own little personality, loved his food and loved being doted on. I was more his human than he was my cat; he definitely ran the show.

He came to me in 2010 during the awful winter we were having here in Ireland. I heard a crying noise outside and so I opened the door. Amazingly, he walked straight in, helped himself to some food and decided to stay! He was spoiled rotten: he had the best food, a spot on my bed, the prize chair in my house but for every ounce of love I gave him, I got it back a thousand times over. He was a sociable little thing with people, always automatically assuming that any visitors were there to see him personally. He wouldn't hesitate in climbing onto them to make a bed on their laps for himself. He wasn't so keen on other male cats, probably because they beat him up all the time and seemed tolerant enough of the female cats, especially the one that insisted on washing him while he was sleeping.

One night, about a year and a half ago, he didn't come home. I knew something was up. He was too much of a petted cat to stay outside at night by himself when he could be curled up on a bed in a nice warm house. I assumed he had got distracted by something and would be home in the morning so went to bed. Something I regret to this day. We found him the following morning, it was evident he had been hit by a car. He was still alive but obviously very sore. Not surprising though was when I put a dish of food under his nose to see if he had an appetite (a lack of one with this lad would have been a sure sign something horrendous was wrong) he tucked in and ate it.

A trip to the vet miraculously revealed no broken bones, but it was obvious his tail was paralysed, something I knew could cause problems with him going to the bathroom. Ginger however, soldiered on. His recovery time was lengthy, he couldn't walk properly and his entire tummy was black from a giant bruise that covered it. I could also tell he was unable to poop easily, so he was on mineral oil for life for that. Gradually though, he regained use of his hind legs, the hunched back he had straightened out and he was a happy little chappy again, albeit one with special needs.

Things were good for a year and then one night I came home from work and I couldn't find him. Ginger was ALWAYS home when I was – again, I knew something was up. He eventually came home by himself and I knew a car had hit him, once again. He seemed perfectly fine but I whisked him to the emergency vet anyway to be on the safe side. She assured me he was fine and gave him a painkiller just in case he deteriorated throughout the night.

Driving home with him I was admittedly upset. After he had been hit the first time, I had still let him out to run around. The worry I had previously had niggling at me in the back of my mind hadn't been there because I had thought it surely couldn't happen him again, yet, here we were.

I didn't know it at the time, but that night the clock started counting down on us. The second accident had happened in August, and then one night in October he was sick. Nothing unusual there – with his constipation sometimes straining could cause him to be sick, but the following morning he collapsed and started screaming, so it was back to the vet he went. They sedated him and gave him a thorough enema, believing him to be badly constipated. I collected him in the evening and brought him home thinking nothing more over it. He had had enemas before. Nothing alarming there, I was sure he was going to be fine. The next day though, I noticed his hind foot was a little turned in and he seemed to be having trouble walking on it and then that night, he collapsed again and was back at the vets again. They thought it was a side effect of the enema.

I wish that had been all it was, he went around the house that night trying to go to the bathroom. It wasn't until the next day we realised what was happening, he was trying to pee and wasn't able to. As an experienced cat owner I know that this usually means end of the road, so with a heavy heart, I brought him back to his vet. By now they were very used to my Ginger boy! They checked him for a blockage, but found none, so they tested his kidneys and found there were failing. I drove back to the vet after mentally preparing myself that I was putting him to sleep, but when I got there and he saw me he, obviously believed he was coming home, purring and rubbing his head along the cat box, so I decided to bring him home for one last night of spoiling with me.

He actually lasted until Sunday, I had thought he might hang in there until Monday but Sunday morning revealed he was wetting himself. The fluid build-up was leaking out of him, and I could tell he was uncomfortable. Everyone said goodbye to him, I cuddled him and brought him back to the surgery and he was placed in my arms for one more cuddle, then I nodded my head and at 3.30 p.m. on October 23, 2016, the vet put him gently to sleep. I cried all the way home and every night for about two weeks.

I tortured myself over his passing, convinced I had missed something or didn't try to do enough at the end. After all – he had been hit twice by cars, why after surviving all that did he have to go? I also remember the day he passed he was outside enjoying the last bit of sunshine in the afternoon and a leaf blew by him, he swatted at it with his paw, this convinced me I had done the wrong thing as he had still been playful. So, a friend of mine mentioned Jackie Weaver and sent me a link to her site and we arranged a meeting over webcam.

Jackie phoned me on a Friday evening, she was wonderfully accommodating and so patient with me. My head was still a mess so it took me a minute to connect what she was saying with Ginger. But she had found him. She said he wasn't a stupid silly cat, more a sweet little follow you around type of cat, which is him exactly.

Jackie told me she had asked him gently why he went to Heaven and she said she felt a cold feeling in her legs, like her back legs were cold and that he wasn't badly injured. For a second I didn't connect with this and must have just looked baffled, but then I remembered his back legs not working after the first accident and then his leg not working right during the week he was ill before passing away. I was mortified I hadn't connected it sooner! His not being badly injured confused me because in my mind he was injured (paralysed tail) but Jackie clarified for me that there was no visible damage done to him and that his face looked perfect. His looks were very important to him and he mentioned how good he looked during the reading several times!

Jackie mentioned several things that convinced me she had found him. She told me he said he never got lost, which is true and how when people visited that he would always behave like they were there to see him and how he liked his food and I always knew when he wanted it – again true! She also talked about digging under a bed cover for something and this one stumped me, it wasn't until afterwards I realised what he had been trying to communicate. When I was in bed at night and he would jump up beside me and if my hands were under the covers and not petting him, he would burrow and claw at the covers until he 'found' them and pulled them out for him to be petted.

At one point during the meeting Jackie started laughing and seemed a little taken aback. She said he was showing her a picture of his – for lack of a politer term – male cat bits! She asked me had I had him for a year or two before neutering him which again, was spot on. Poor Jackie! She said never during a reading had an animal decided to show her that mental image. I explained that he would always get into fights, which led to vet visits, so I neutered him hoping it would take the aggressiveness out of him. To be honest, he couldn't fight his way out of a paper bag so he always came off the worse but what I hadn't counted on was other male cats would still pick on him, and he still got beaten up. I always knew he never forgave me for organising 'the op' for him!

The other part of the meeting was what really convinced me. Jackie said she was getting a strange image of a door, and in the door were some rectangles that were getting filled in. For a second I was confused and then I remembered what I had been doing that day. There is a door in my shed that had eight glass squares in it. A while ago the door had slammed and two of the panes near the bottom had broken, but I never filled in the gaps because I left it as a type of cat flap for him to come in and out of. Well that very day I had been covering up these rectangles in the door. Looks like I had had some company while I was doing it.

Near the end of the meeting was what cinched it for me though. Jackie again looked confused and had a little laugh to herself before asking me. She said she heard, "sniff my fur" and asked if it made any sense. I'm sure my face was a picture. Ginger and I had a thing where he would sit beside me, and if I made a sniffing noise he would put his head back for kisses on his head. That day I had asked him that if he came through to try to mention it if he could.

The final validation Jackie provided me with was to ask me if I made lots of cups of tea! Nothing surprising there, we all do. However, then she said she could see me at work making a cup of tea at a desk and then wiping it down. Well, I take tea to work, I make it at my desk from the flask and then before I leave for the evening, I wipe down my desk. How wonderful that I have been getting visited at work as well!

Throughout the reading, Jackie told me that he was pretty chilled out about his passing and that he was totally at peace. She assured me I had done the right thing and that Ginger was resting now, while obviously popping in to see me. It brought me an immeasurable sense of calm and reassurance. I know that he is with me, and waiting for me on the other side too. I saw this reading as proof that the other side was true now. Jackie pinpointed too many things that no one else would have known or could have known, especially the "sniff my fur" thing!

I am normally an extremely private person but by publishing this story I hope it will bring peace and reassurance to others. If anyone is going through the same doubt and grief that I did I do recommend reaching out to Jackie. You will be treated with kindness, warmth and compassion. Although I will miss him forever, after our reading I actually had my first night's sleep in a month! The communication really helped ease my heart and to absolutely know that one day, Ginge and I will be together again, is immeasurable.

*****

Vanessa and her cats Sugar and Muffin

Sugar and Muffin were brother and sister, both
tabbies, but with completely different personalities;
Sugar was a gentle lady and kept her beautiful
'kitten' looks right up until she passed at almost aged
21. She was what I like to call my 'Angel sent from
Heaven'. Muffin, on the other hand was a typical
boy, always getting into scrapes and making his
presence known from day one, right up until the day
he passed, at almost aged 23. He was however loved
equally as much, and we became particularly close
over the last two years spent on our own without
Sugar.

I was never what you would call a 'cat lover'; I
remember the family having a dog (Prince) when I
was a young girl, who passed when we were both
aged eleven. Prince was a lovely, sweet dog who I
still think of fondly almost 40 years later.

I grew up with my Mum (a single parent) and my
grandparents. When I was 15, my grandparents
moved to Wales, so mum rented a small flat for us in
Liverpool. We lived there for the next 11 years. My
grandad passed away from lung cancer when I was
21, so my grandma moved back to be with us in
Liverpool. The three of us (Grandma, mum and
daughter) were inseparable. My grandma died
suddenly from a heart attack when I was 26 years'
old. Both Mum and I were devastated, as you can
imagine.

Mum had kidney problems and had to have major
surgery in 1995; she knew she would be in hospital
for a few weeks and one day she went out for a loaf
of bread, and came home with a kitten! She said this
kitten would keep me company while she was in

hospital, and boy was she right! We called her 'Meggie' after my grandma, and that cat did not leave my side all the time Mum was in hospital. It turns out that Meggie was actually a boy, but that's another story! Fortunately, Mum survived the operation and came home.

I had a good job at the time, so I decided we needed a fresh start. I bought a house (I'm still there now, 23 years' later) and my Mum came with me. The two of us were already best friends, but now that we had no family left, our bond became stronger – we were practically joined at the hip. We both had partners over the years, and I was briefly married (disaster, long story!) but for the most part, we were both single.

Meggie could not settle in my new hous,and to this day, I don't know why. After a few weeks, she ran away and never came back. Mum and I were distraught and put posters up, traipsed the streets and phoned all the cat rescues, but to no avail. I felt she wasn't coming back and I still hope to this day that she found another family, and was loved as much as we loved her.

I had to tell you about Meggie as she was the reason that Sugar and Muffin came into our lives. (This was back in 1995.)

One day, a few weeks' later, a man from the Cats Protection League knocked at our door and asked us if we would be interested in taking in a pair of six-week-old kittens? They knew about Meggie going missing and all our efforts to try to find her. They had Sugar and Muffin with them; I was hesitant at first as I will still hoping Meggie would come back,but, from the minute they were let out of their basket, they made themselves right at home! They had been found in an alley in a bin bag – I have no idea how people can be so wicked. Here were two tiny tabby and white kittens. Whilst at our house, the Cat's Protection man received a phone call from his colleague to let him know they had been offered a home elsewhere! He told us what had been said, but with our look of, 'Don't you dare take them away from us' they were officially adopted by us there and then. We called the boy Muffin and the girl, Sugar.

Muffin was Mum's cat and Sugar was mine; but we were one big happy family.

Then on 29th November 1999 my world crashed when Mum died suddenly from a massive brain haemorrhage; she was only 53. The day after she died, I didn't want to get out of bed and buried my head under the duvet. The next minute the duvet was dragged off me and there were two sets of cats' eyes looking at me as if to say, 'Excuse me, but we're hungry!' From that moment on, they were my reason for carrying on. They were house cats and we lived our lives blissfully together.

They became my best friends and although Muffin was loved equally, and I met his every demand, I had a special bond with Sugar because we would spend almost every moment together. She even slept in my bed with her head on my pillow. She would lick my tears away if I was upset, and she would never leave my side if I was ill. I used to sing her to sleep at night; then one night when she was around 19, she started to tap my mouth with her paws and I couldn't understand why. After a few nights I realised, she had gone deaf and she couldn't hear me sing any longer! She carried on and enjoyed her life to the full. One memory sticks in my mind when she decided to chew the Christmas tree, one of those artificial ones. I did not realise she was actually eating it, until one day she gave me a real fright, when I saw a pine needle sticking out of her backside. I carefully pulled it but it wouldn't budge, so we ended up at the vets. They had to operate on her to extract it, as it got wrapped around inside her intestines. That was the end of the Christmas trees in our house!

I had to have Sugar put to sleep on 18th March 2016; when she was almost 21. She became ill over a period of about a week with breathing problems. Then one evening, her back legs buckled under her and she couldn't get up. The vet came round the next day and simply said to me, 'If she were mine, I would let her go'. I was with her when she died. We were on the rug in front of the fire (her favourite place) and it was the most peaceful ending, although I was heartbroken, and always will be.

I wondered how I was going to carry on without my little Angel, and then Muffin jumped onto my knee as if to say, 'You still have me!' For the next two years he had my undivided attention and ruled the house! I have to admit that although he was of senior years, he still got told off on occasions as he was a bit of a careless live-wire to say the least!

One of the many scrapes he got into when he was younger, was when I had a new washing machine plumbed in. The guy fitted the machine and left; but I couldn't find Muffin anywhere and the next minute I heard this howling (like a banshee!) and realised that he was stuck behind the washing machine! I don't know where I found the strength from as they have heavy concrete weights in them, but somehow I got the machine out and Muffin ran past me like 'Flash Gordon'. I checked he was okay, which he was but he stayed upstairs for the rest of the day. I shouldn't laugh really but he steadfastly refused to come down!

Muffin had lost a lot of weight but became very ill around two days before I had him put to sleep (22nd February 2018) but he refused to give up. He was disoriented and tried to get around, but I decided it was time, and made the dreaded phone call to the vet – he was booked in for the following day. In the middle of the night he took a turn for the worse and I had to call the vet out and she put him to sleep. His passing was not so straight forward as his blood pressure was low and at one point, he tried to get up and walk off, but he was too weak. I knew it was time, although he was trying to be strong to the end. Typical Muffin! Again, I was left heartbroken, but thankful that he lived to the grand old age of almost 23.

I always promised myself I would contact an animal psychic at some point, but I felt it was too raw when I lost Sugar because it wasn't expected. I'm a strong believer in the after-life, but wanted some sort of confirmation/reassurance that they were okay, and with my family. Boy, did I get that from Jackie!

I searched on the internet about six months after Sugar passed, and Jackie's name popped up, so I kept her details for when I was ready. About a week before Muffin passed, Jackie's name kept popping up on my Twitter feed; how spooky! We made the appointment for around three weeks after Muffin passed and it was the best thing I ever did.

Muffin came through first; Jackie described him to a 'tee'; big personality, not shy, loves attention... yep, that's Muffin! She even described with great detail about how he became ill and passed – only someone who was actually talking to Muffin could have known. I was so proud of him when she mentioned the fact that he was still *determined* to the very end. I also got goose bumps when she mentioned that Christmas was a big day for him; I knew it was probably going to be his last Christmas, so we (my friend and me) made an extra special fuss of him. He got lots of toys, treats, his own Christmas hat, and his own dinner – turkey and gravy! I then gave him a groom with his big brush, and I'll always remember what a special day it was for him. I even posted a photo of us both on Twitter (something I never do!).

I asked Jackie if Muffin was okay as I felt guilty for telling him off when he was naughty. She reassured me that he wasn't bothered whatsoever, and to let it go! We also chatted about his 'not straight forward' ending; Jackie made me giggle when she repeated from him, 'What did you expect from me?' We both laughed as this is so true; it was never going to be easy! I've thought that I've seen him a couple of times in the house, just a fleeting shadow. Jackie reassured me I'm not going mad; he's letting me know he's okay and is still around me.

We had a little break, and then we moved on to Sugar; Jackie confirmed it was her… a very bright lady, like a little gentle angel who slept on the bed with me! She also mentioned that when Sugar was comfortable on my knee when I was sat on the sofa, that I wouldn't move for hours as I did not want to disturb her! Sugar also mentioned that she 'escaped' once but didn't go far. Yes she did, the one and only time. I happened to look out of the window and there she was sitting on the garden wall. I eventually coaxed her back in, and breathed a huge sigh of relief. The funny thing is; I had totally forgotten all about it, so the only person who could have told her was, Sugar!

Jackie also knew exactly how Sugar became ill; she knew about her breathing problems and heart issues. She said it was likely that a blood clot from her heart had travelled and affected her back legs too.

A few days after Sugar passed, I was driving with the car window down and the tiniest white feather I have ever seen flew right onto the dashboard. I'm convinced this was Sugar and Jackie confirmed this; she also said Sugar has visited me several times in my dreams, and Sugar was very clear about this. I couldn't believe what I was hearing as I had thought it was my imagination! I distinctly recall three occasions when I've woken up in the middle of the night, and I could actually 'hear//feel' (it's hard to describe) Sugar jumping onto the bed, and snuggling down with me. I now know these were visitations from her.

A few days after the readings with Jackie, one Sunday morning, exactly two years to the day since Sugar passed, I was lying in bed, dozing, just about to get up. Suddenly, an ornament that was on my windowsill, did a wobble as if been moved by something, and then I 'felt' Sugar jump from the windowsill on to my bed! She then went on to do some patting on my head with her little paws! It was simply incredible. If I hadn't had my reading with Jackie, I would have dismissed this as 'my imagination' but I'm convinced it was her letting me know she's still around. She must have known it was the anniversary of her death, and that I was feeling particularly low, especially with Muffin passing.

Since the day Muffin passed, I've been asking him to send me a white feather; he kept me waiting until 25 days later! The day after Sugar's 'visit', I was leaving the house and I was locking the doors in the kitchen and I said, 'Come on Muffin, why haven't you sent me a white feather yet?' Then something caught my eye; right next to the one and only daffodil that's bloomed so far in my garden this year, was a single, solitary white feather! I don't know how it managed to stay put as we were having gale force winds, but there it was. I ran outside and quickly picked it up; I then thanked Muffin, and had a little cry.

Both these events have happened since my readings with Jackie, and I'm sure she may have given them a little nudge to cheer me up!

If I wasn't convinced that our beloved animal family live on in Heaven before, I most certainly am now having spoken to Jackie; it's such a reassuring feeling to know that they have 'survived' death and are waiting for us to join them!

I don't expect to arrive at a point in my life where I am 'alright' with the fact that they are no longer with me (physically) but through Jackie, I have been reminded that I have been so lucky and blessed to have loved, and been loved that much, by these two adorable souls. Also, the fact that our story is being memorialised in this book makes me feel so proud, and I know they will be too.

*****

Emma and her dog Max

My life changed forever on 6th April 2013. It was a lovely sunny day and it was the day I became mum to Max, a very beautiful Sprollie – a springer/collie cross breed, who was around seven-years-old. I first saw him in a photograph on a website and to be honest, it wasn't a flattering picture of him but I just knew in my heart straight away, I had to be his mum. He was quite bedraggled, very thin, and had a look of sadness in his eyes. The re-homing centre had no history of his background. I checked what their opening times were as I was determined to go and see him.

I remember going to the rescue centre and looking around for him. At first I couldn't find him and I was getting a little upset, because I thought someone else had maybe beaten me to him. However, as I walked around the corner to the last section, there he was. I stopped in my tracks. What a handsome boy! He was woofing at me but as I stopped in front of him, we looked into each other's eyes for what seemed longer than usual. He stopped barking, but his lip was stuck to the top side of his teeth so he had this really funny grin! That was it for me. True love at first sight! I told him where I lived, and about the country park nearby where I would be taking him to. I chatted to him about his new bed and all the toys that were waiting at home for him.

We then got to meet 'person-to-person', we had a lovely walk and spent time together. Arrangements were made there and then to adopt him. I remember that he stood on his back two legs and put his front paws over my arm. I think that was he saying how he wanted to be with me too! I am convinced he understood every word I was saying to the staff that day, and he knew that I wanted to take him home. That was it! Our fates were sealed there and then!

The Dogs Trust had called him Elvis (I think it was because of his lip sticking to his top teeth) but I renamed him Max. I had always wanted a son called Max. Actually, his full title was Maxwell James after a holiday romance with a boy I met at Torquay in 1985 when I was 15!

My sister came with me to pick Max up on that Saturday morning. They have a system where all rehomed dogs are picked up at the same time. As all the dogs were brought round to their new families, I remember my sister just bursting into tears. She thought it was so wonderful to see those dogs given a second chance. She had never experienced this before – I think it hit home with her that there is this other side to life where animals need a chance, and some good luck in their lives for a change.

We got him home, he ran continuously around my house. He constantly jumped on the sofa and onto my bed. I am sure he was hoping that he would be allowed onto both. After a few months he was! It was now just a case of us both spending time getting used to each other, and learning a routine. I had the following week off work, and we had such a lovely time. He settled in quite quickly and thinking about it, I am sure he just needed confirmation that I really did 'have his back' and that he could trust me.

A couple of weeks after getting him, an odd thing happened... A representative from the re-homing centre called round to check on his progress. I am sure Max recognised her and where she was from. He panicked, zoomed past her out of the front door, and ran into a neighbour's house four-doors-down hiding under her bed. I can only presume that he thought she was there to take him back? Like I'd ever let that happen – not in a million years! I didn't know my neighbour until then, but I did after that!

Every night for the first few weeks, I used to get Max into the back of my car and drive him around the estate, just to get him used to travelling and knowing he was always coming back to his home. My neighbours must have thought I was potty. I did it because I knew absolutely nothing of his past, so I thought it was best to start from scratch with him.

I realised early on that I had a very intelligent boy, but with a mischievous side to his character. When I look back now, he seemed to be testing my love and loyalty in the beginning. Three months in, it was the height of summer, and we were walking along the old disused canal footpath near to where we live. There wasn't another living soul about, only us – apart from the ducks. The canal was covered in a green algae film – yuck, although rather picturesque.

Max stopped in his tracks and looked at me for a few seconds. I just knew what he was going to do. As quickly I uttered the words, 'No please don't', regardless, and in a flash, he had. He'd jumped into the canal and disappeared under the green film. Talk about my heart stopping and panic ensuing; It is a six foot drop from the path to the water level, and really not a good place to be. Now, I am not a big woman by any means, and don't ask me how I did it, but I managed to pull him back and up by his extendable lead and harness, and haul him out. (This was no mean feat, as by that time he was now 36 kilo's in weight (because I had been feeding him up and giving him treats to win him over.)

Well, if you could have seen the state of him! He was completely covered in this black tarry film that stunk to high heaven. All I could see were these two sparkly brown eyes glistening through the muck! With relief, I laughed and said, 'I can't believe you just did that' and we went to a nearby river so I could wash off as much of it as I could. It took a week to entirely rid him of that stinky smell. I have to say, I laughed and laughed with him about that for weeks afterwards, and tried constantly to be one step ahead of him and his thoughts.

We would go walking every day, whatever the weather. He had the body of a collie but he definitely had a Springer Spaniel brain. His 'thing' was to disappear into bushes and bring out whatever was in there. Sometimes annoyingly, he would find a discarded kebab or suchlike. I can't tell you the amount of times we were at the vet because he had a stomach issue. The problem was, I could never get a kebab or chips off him once he'd got it. He scoffed it, wrapping paper included!

I absolutely loved my time with Max. I'd try to come home from work early, or take a day's holiday just to spend time with him. He was just a lovely, lovely boy, with a beautiful personality. Our bond was growing stronger by the minute. Whatever room I was in, he would be there, making sure he could see me. I'd talk non-stop to him all the time, telling him all my thoughts and troubles. I didn't realise just how much I did talk (probably too much) until Max pointed that out to Jackie during our reading! So, yes, he was listening!

I lost both my parents whilst I had Max and I'd talk to him about how I felt. Sometimes I'd get upset remembering my childhood, and how time passes so quickly. Max was there constantly for me. To be honest, I don't know what I would have done without him. He would just sit and listen, and paw my arm as if to say, 'It's okay mum – I understand'. We spent many an hour on the settee cuddled up.

From day one, it was obvious that Max had problems with his joints and back too. The supplements I was giving him didn't seem to be working as well anymore. One day, he couldn't climb the stairs so I knew at that point it was serious. After a couple of trips to the vets, and after everything she gave him and had suggested, were not working, I watched him deteriorate very quickly over the period of a week.

My sister and I took him to the vet again on the Monday, and after a scan, we were told said there was nothing more they could do. He now had severe arthritis, not just in his joints, but in his spine too. He was still unconscious and he didn't wake up ever again. I lost my precious boy on 12th February 2018 at 3.15pm. I was utterly devastated. For a long time, I cried every single day for my boy. Some people might say that's ridiculous, but I loved him and I always will. Loss is loss, and he was my boy who I loved with all of my heart.

After that, I couldn't cope with his empty bed, his collar and lead hanging up, his toys in his toy box – I'm sure most of you can relate to that. Max had lived with me, shared my bed, listened to my non-stop chattering, everything – then all of a sudden the house was empty; That horrible empty silence that greeted me when I come home from work, instead of that fun bundle of fur that gave me a wonderful enthusiastic and loving greeting. He made my house a home. Everything had changed in an instant.

I was struggling and it wasn't getting any easier. I can't stand it when people say 'time is a great healer'. Well, it was not doing so for me! My sister suggested bereavement counselling, but it wasn't counselling that I needed. I understand the stages of grieving. I'd been through it often enough lately. No, I just wanted to know my Maxi was safe, loved and happy and that he understood what had happened.

This is how Jackie came into my life... We met on a lovely warm summer's day. I felt at ease straight away with her calming influence toward me. I only gave her minimal information about Max before the reading, which included a photograph of him.

Now I can only give you my experience of receiving a reading from Jackie, but I have to tell you – Max came through immediately and the things he talked about just blew me away. He told Jackie that he had come to me because his previous owner had passed away, so he could relate to me losing my parents. Wow!

He described to Jackie how I would put my nose to his every day, and tell him how much I loved him. How I would stroke the white stripe on his nose that went to his forehead with one finger and he'd close his eyes! He relayed to Jackie how every day when I came home from work, I would say to him, 'What have you been up to while I've been gone?' He enlightened both of us saying he would think, 'What do you think I was doing? I was waiting for you!' He was recalling everything about our daily lives together whilst he was still on earth. I would always tell him we were a team, and this was something else he mentioned several times during the reading.

While this is truly fantastic in itself, what really has changed things for me is that he gave information to

Jackie about things I have done and/or am doing for him after his passing. There has been an advertisement on TV recently with the song, It must be Love, by Madness. I sang it all the way through and said out- loud, 'Maxi this is our song forever'. Ever since then, every time I hear that song, I think of my Max. He told Jackie about our special song, bless him.

He reminisced about how every day I used to put my slippers next to his bed and ask him to look after them until I get home. There is one validation that has had me in stitches and laughing since the reading. He told Jackie how he thought my broad Manchester accent is hilarious. How he would laugh to himself when he would hear me shouting 'Max, Maxi' at the top of my voice. What makes this truly remarkable for me is, (and what I haven't told you), is that I got Max from The Dogs Trust in Liverpool. I had a Scouse dog! All the way through our five years together I always used to say to him, 'Maxi, you're a Manc' now, you can't have that Scouse accent anymore'. How funny is that? I have laughed ever since about that particular detail. (For readers not familiar with British places; Scouse is a nickname for people from Liverpool, as Manc is for us from Manchester.)

All through the reading he kept re-iterating his love for me, and mine for him. Truly wonderful! I realised I really had got a dog with a terrific sense of humour, super intelligent and is still with me to this day – it is just that I cannot physically see him, that's all!

I don't, and have never used social media, or social networking things. I'm one of the remaining 'old school' gang. So, unless Jackie has been bugging my house for the last five years, then I cannot explain how she would know those details of my Maxi and me, and our lives together. It was the truly personal details of our unique relationship we had built, that no one else would know. It was validation, after validation, after validation. Every single thing she passed onto me from Max was correct. It truly was.

What Jackie has given me is peace. Peace and the knowledge that life really does go on after we leave Earth, and that we will all be re-united with our loved ones, and our pets, when the time comes. I am no longer afraid.

My sister and I had often pondered at our mother's graveside, wondering if this was it, and if there was nothing more after we die. Well, I no longer live with that fear now as Jackie has given me validation.

Not only has Jackie brought me peace, but she also brought me my Max. I know he is still with me every day, and that fills my heart with joy.

Just one final thought – people should never underestimate that their animal is of a lesser intelligence and doesn't understand them, or doesn't have emotions just like we do. They really, really do, and hearing it 'straight' from Max himself, has shown me that, and more. Thank you Jackie, lots of love from Emma and Max xx.

*****

Judy and her horse Kali

Kali is my 34-year-old chestnut 3/4 Arabian mare. I have owned her for nearly 31 years. This is our story.

When I was a young girl I was obsessed with horses, and rode as often as I could at a riding school, and on my babysitter's horses. All I dreamt about was that one day, I would have my very own horse. At the time that Kali came into my life, I had been reading over and over the 'Jinny' books by Patricia Leitch. They were about a young girl, of my age at the time, and her beloved Chestnut Arabian Mare Shantih. I was hooked. I was adamant that I would one day have a horse just like Shantih.

I had decided that I wanted to work with horses as a career, but to help persuade me into a different line of work, my parents said that they would buy one for me as long as I didn't go into a horse career, and that I could find somewhere to keep it. Easy decision! With my determination, I soon found through word of mouth, a lady called Sheila, who was willing to share her field with me for £8 a week. Now all I had to do was to find a suitable horse. I scoured the ads in the papers as this was before the days of the internet, and I soon found what I was looking for... A beautiful chestnut 3/4 Arabian mare with a flaxen mane and tail called Kalico.

She is known to me as Kali. My goodness she was stunning. At 15 hands 3" she was bigger than I was used to. She was coming up to four-years-old, and had recently been broken in to ride. Probably not the wisest choice for someone that had little experience with youngsters, but I knew I just had to have her. So with the deal done, she was delivered to me the following weekend. I was so excited seeing her coming down the ramp of the horse box, and then being led into the field. It was the best day of my life, and I couldn't have been any happier.

So for the next 30 odd years, Kali was my life. We didn't do any shows or that sort of thing, we were just content to hack out and ride in the field. To be honest, just merely being in her presence was wonderful. I was always with her, well as much as time would allow anyway. School days were the best as there was so much free time, but going into full time work meant that I could not spend as much time with her. To this day I feel bad about that, but that's life.

Over the years we moved a few times, and have been settled not far from my home for the past 10 years or so. She knows my routines, and is always waiting for me by the gate as she knows the sound of my car travelling along the lane. Each time I see her I am filled with love. She has been the best friend a girl could ask for, and has been my comfort through some really rotten times in my life, including the death of my mother. I'd put my arms around her neck, sob into her mane, and she would just look at me with her big brown eyes and I'd feel that everything would be okay as long as I had her. She had the ability to heal. I just don't know what I would do without her.

We've been extremely lucky throughout her life as she has had no serious health issues. We've had bouts of mud fever like most other horse owners and COPD, (condition where dust/mould spores etc. affects their lungs) but living outside 24/7 with open access to a stable and suitable feeding has kept that under control. So really, the two of us have just coasted through life without a care in the world. About five years ago she started to get early signs of arthritis. She was a little stiffer in her movements, but with joint supplements etc. she seemed content enough. I retired her, and only occasionally rode her bareback around the field, and led her in the field to keep her moving.

A couple of months ago I arrived at the field to find her not at the gate as usual, but down on the ground. I instantly panicked, but saw her raise her head so I knew that she was alive. Phew! I went over to her and she seemed calm enough, and was happy to have an apple and some Polo sweets. This had happened about eight months previously, but when I had returned with help 20 minutes later she was on the far side of the field grazing!

So this time, I thought that I would go and get ready for work, and check on her again on my way to work some half hour later. I found that she hadn't got up, but she still seemed calm and quite happy, so I popped into work to do the important jobs but asked if I could leave to go and see her again. This time she was up and about grazing, but didn't seem to want her breakfast. I had a feeling of unease, so decided to call the vet. By the time the vet came she had eaten her breakfast, so that was a good thing. The vet checked her over and couldn't find anything really wrong, so put it down to her arthritis. She was injected with an anti- inflammatory and painkiller and prescribed painkilling/anti-inflammatory powders for the foreseeable future, so that she would manage more comfortably.

The vet told me to be prepared, because with a horse of such an age, the end was getting closer. She said I might need to put her to sleep before the winter, or she might go on for another few years, time would tell. Even though I knew this would happen one day, hearing those words devastated me, and I was a mess for days trying to deal with it. Every time I saw Kali I'd be sobbing and tell her again and again how much I loved her. She seemed sad which made me even sadder. It really was awful but then I contacted Jackie.

Being an intuitive spiritual person anyway, I felt guided to research for a reputable animal communicator. I had in the past done a horse communication course with great success, but with it being my own horse, my own emotions were getting in the way, and I could feel nothing but despair. I had actually given one of Jackie's books to a dear friend a year or so ago who had just lost her cat, because I thought it would help with the grieving process. So I looked up Jackie's website and made an appointment. Bless her, she was able to do the reading for me a few days later. I was thrilled as I had so many questions to ask. I wrote a list as and when I thought of them.

The day came, and Jackie rang on time and immediately put me at ease. She was so friendly. She told me about Kali's personality, saying that she wasn't a nutty chestnut like they are renowned for being, but that she was safe. She told Jackie about the sheep that have broken into her field a couple of times. Now how would Jackie have known that?! She was able to tell me before I'd even asked, about things that I wanted to know, that Kali was happy and content, she knew I loved her deeply, and that she was my world, and my best friend.

Kali told Jackie that she was just having an 'off day' the day that I had called the vet. She had a bit of stomach ache, nothing more and that she was fine and could still trot and canter. She so can! We have a race every day from one end of the field to the other — she always wins and looks round at me as if to say, 'Come on slowcoach' which makes me smile every time. Even though her gait is not what it used to be, she was not suffering. Jackie did pick up that she has Cushings disease (a disease relating to the pituitary gland) but that it doesn't bother her, although she'd like to be clipped soon before it gets too hot. (The disease often makes shedding their winter coat not so easy.) Kali described clippers as scissors with a machine, which made me laugh. Kali knew I had been thinking about it, but had been worrying as I'd never clipped her before, and wasn't sure how she'd react. As it turned out, she was an angel, and I didn't even have to tie her up! When my husband and I had finished the job, Kali trotted off, did a little buck, looked round at us, and neighed as if to say, 'Thank you'.

There was also a day recently when I found her laid down in the sun, my heart did start to race, but she looked up when she saw me, and then got to her feet. Being in a calmer place of mind I picked up that she was deliberately showing me, 'Look Mum, see I can get up so there is no need to worry.' because one of my questions to Jackie had been, 'was she afraid to lie down if she was having trouble getting up?' Jackie had responded that she was fine but was just more careful these days doing so. Bless Kali. She's so clever.

Since Jackie's reading I have been different, she's given me a gift in deciding to not have Kali put to sleep yet, and to just live day by day, and as Kali put it, what will be will be! She is not afraid, that is a human condition and, when the time comes, I'll know. So that is exactly what we are doing, living day by day. Since I've changed my thoughts to positive ones, she has perked up too. I think when she was sad she was picking up on my sadness. Now we spend all our time living in the moment, going for walks, just hanging out, grooming (she likes to position herself around me showing me exactly what spot to do next) and I even read to her.

I have been studying horse communication again, and our bond in this short time since Jackie's reading, has grown even stronger. I will be forever grateful for that. Kali and I have also decided on a spiritual sign between us (poppies) so that when I see one/them I'll know her energy will come close, and I will send the recognition to her. I thought this apt, as not only is 'Poppy' one of her nicknames, but it's also about remembrance. Since deciding on this sign, I'm seeing them all over the place, and in the strangest of places. I've been told that Kali is already showing me that we can communicate whilst she's still here on Earth when we are apart, as well as when she'll be on the other side. Every time I see one, I am filled with love for my beautiful horse, who has not only been my best friend, but as I realise now through Jackie, a teacher too.

Horses show you how to live at one with the world and to just be. I know I'll be lost without her, but I am so grateful to Jackie as I will be able to find peace when the time comes, knowing that Kali loves me as much as I love her, and that we will always be connected. Thank you Jackie

Over to me, Jackie, for a minute. Judy and I were delighted to share about Kali's reading in my magazine 'Animal Communication' column. We hoped it would bring peace to others with older horses, and try to help guide people to try and live for the day, and enjoy every day that you get. That time did come for Kali to pass and these are the words sent to me from Judy...

Hi Jackie,

I hope you are well. Just thought I'd tell you that I had to say goodbye to Kali yesterday. I would love an afterlife reading with you in the near future. I am very upset right now. I was with her to the end stroking her and kissing her. I am so thankful for what your reading gave me as, because of it, I was able, to be happy for the whole summer without worrying, so we had the best summer ever. Thank you, Judy. x

*****

Kathy and Mark's dog Angel.

Our beloved retired greyhound Bonzo, who we had very sadly lost on 18th September 2014, had hand-picked our beautiful new retired greyhound Angel on a spirit reading with Jackie. He had told us that he thought that we would get another greyhound and that this time, it would be a girl and that she would have dots on her face! After losing Bonzo, we had been volunteering to walk the retired greyhounds, and funnily enough, a very pretty dog had already caught my husband Mark's eye.

Whilst all the other greyhounds had come dashing over for us to take out for a walk, Mark had noticed this one dog who had just stayed lying on her bed looking at us... which made her stand out. The next time we visited the kennels again to volunteer, this dog had been outside, and had been jumping higher than we had ever seen a dog jump before EVER and again, she stood out! When we got home, something kept making us think about this beautiful greyhound as we had noticed that she also had dots all over her. We started to wonder if she could be the one that Bonzo had spoken about in his reading. When we looked at her details on the greyhound website, we found out her retired name was Angel. We felt this was like a sign – we had a gut feeling this was her!

The next time we visited the kennels, we asked if we could take Angel out for a few hours, and she seemed so excited. We took her out in the car to take her for a nice walk and when we arrived at our destination, she walked straight up to me and licked me on the face! We both thought this was just so sweet and endearing, and again a sign. Out of all the dogs we had taken out, she was the only one that had immediately shown us affection, and by the time we arrived back home, we had already made our minds up that she was the one. It felt like she was a female version of Bonzo, and so on 10th January 2015, Angel became our new dog, and came to her forever home with us.

Angel was adorable, and we were so happy that we had got her, but it soon became apparent that far from being a female version of sensible Bonzo – she was actually a very excitable dog, and completely different to Bonzo's gentle, laid back placid nature. Angel had a habit of barking her head off with excitement. When she met other dogs, she would be so excited that she would just launch herself at them to as if to say, 'Hi', The main difference was that Bonzo, who had previously been fostered by a squaddie for nine months before we got him, had a pretty good understanding of living in a home before we got him. Whereas Angel, had never been in a home before, and just found everything so exciting. It was literally like having a giant puppy to train from scratch.

After having such a calm, placid dog, who hardly ever barked (but when he did sounded like the Barry

White of the dog world) to now having this super charged ball of energy, complete with a high pitched bark, just took us completely by surprise. We did not know how to handle her and calm her down. We were also worried that as we were still really grieving after Bonzo, that Angel might feel second best, as we now know that they can hear and understand what we say and think. We didn't ever want her to feel like that. We therefore decided to have a chat with Jackie and Angel, to see if she was settling in okay, and to try and tackle a few teething problems.

As it was also approaching Bonzo's anniversary and we still missed him so much, we were desperate to have a chat with him again, so we booked a double chat. Angel got to chat first and told Jackie that she is a very upbeat and happy girl and wants for nothing. We knew this was her immediately. She told Jackie that she can still run and, soooo fast. Jackie told us she could feel a real gentle essence about her. This was all true, Angel has such a lovely gentle nature; she is just one big excited girl. She also showed Jackie an image of her sitting, and Jackie said that she sits funny, pushing her legs through underneath. We knew exactly what she meant, as it does make us laugh how she sits. We know greyhounds can't sit for long because of their long legs so they do look a bit peculiar, but Angel really does have a funny sitting position.

Angel then went on to tell Jackie 'I'm a wise old bird' which made us giggle. She said, 'I'm switched on, and can take things in my stride and learn'. Again this is true as we had recently started to teach her to 'stay' and 'come' and she has picked it up so quickly and we were really proud of her. She told Jackie that when she moved in, she settled in really quickly and made us laugh by sharing her thought, 'This will do me, thank you very much!' She really had completely made herself at home and it was as if she was lady of the manor. We loved the fact that she felt so at home. Angel told Jackie that the 'Car is mine!' and said that she is a bit like a 'kid in a sweet shop' when she is in the car.

Angel then went on to tell Jackie that she is actually quite hardy, but that we can molly- coddle her if we like, and also that she always looked good in black (from in her racing days). Guess what colour her next coat was that we bought her? Yes and she actually looked really good in black with her white colouring.

Jackie said she actually has a lovely way about her, that every day is exciting to her, and that she is so upbeat and happy. I don't think we have ever seen such an excitable and happy dog before, so Jackie had her summed up completely.

We asked Jackie to ask Angel why, when she met other dogs, did she leap in at them? Angel showed Jackie her tail wagging, and said that it was just ignorance of not knowing what to do. She declared that she hasn't done any harm at all, but that we had governed the situation. She pointed out to Jackie that there has been one dog that has been showing her what to do. We think this is a neighbours little dog as whenever Angel meets this certain dog, she is pretty calm and walks really nicely beside him. "I just so like to play" Angel enthused and Jackie said she could see Angel showing her with legs everywhere. She said her excitement gets the better of her, but that she is not trying to hurt or bite a dog. Angel told Jackie, 'I know it's stupid behaviour, but I can't control myself. I don't know what to do, I don't know what to do!' This was a relief to know that she didn't want to harm any dogs when she jumped in, but that she was just naïve of how to approach the situation which was all completely new to her. She then randomly went on to say, 'I'm quite big you know!' which made us giggle.

She mentioned Aoife which is my brother's little dog (who also used to be Bonzo's best buddy) and that Aoifa was asserting a bit of authority with her and telling her to 'back off' when she jumped in to say, 'Hello!' She said to tell her 'Respect' when she next meets Aoifa and to feed them both treats as it will distract them! We did try this and it did seem to help and Angel got her wish for extra treats too!

Angel then went on to mention a robin. Whenever we went away on our weekends or trips (which Bonzo loved doing) we always used to see a little robin. Jackie confirmed that this is sent by spirit, so it is lovely to know our lovely Bonzo is around us still, especially on our trips away. Angel went on to tell Jackie that she can be having a wee and that something will happen, or catch her eye, and she will get up and go! 'Wee and go, wee and go!' She said that every minute is important! She is funny, and it really does sum her up! She is just literally so full of life.

We had taken Angel on a retired greyhound fun day not that long after we had got her, and Angel told Jackie about this and said that she had been remarkably well behaved on the fun day. In fact, a lot of the volunteers had to ask if it was actually Angel that we had with us, as they weren't used to seeing her on all four feet, as she is usually jumping and bouncing up and down. We entered her into the assault course and she won third prize, and we were so proud of her and how she had behaved the entire day.

We asked Jackie how she is health wise, and as usual, Jackie said she did not diagnose, however, Angel had indicated that she hasn't got any health issues like diarrhoea etc. We had noticed that she had been doing some reverse sneezing ever since we got her. (This was concerning us as reverse sneezing was one of the first symptoms with Bonzo when he first became ill before we lost him, so we wanted to check if everything was okay with Angel.) She explained that some sand went up her nose when she had been a racing dog, and that her right nostril had been damaged by the sand, but there was nothing wrong with her breathing, which was very reassuring. She also showed Jackie that she had a broken canine tooth. We hadn't noticed this before, but sure enough she has a broken canine. She said to Jackie, 'In fact I'm fine!' and if we are worried about the reverse sneezing, to get her up and it will stop, but not to panic. Sure enough this has worked.

Angel then started to speak about Christmas and showed Jackie an image of holly. She said "I'm going to love Christmas!"

We asked Jackie to ask if Angel is happy in her new home, to which she smiles and said "Life is solitude. This is me! I'm here, everything is here for me!" "I'm ever so good, and not a pest!" Hmmm.... The pest part we might have to challenge Angel about, as on occasions she has run off and chewed some of my baseball caps and really nice work shoes, but on the whole she has settled in so well and is really good in that she is not destructive considering everything is all so new to her living in a home, after being in the kennels for so long. She told Jackie that when she makes a "Hmmm Hmmm" noise to us, that it is her talking to us, which made us smile again.

Jackie then asked if we had taken her place where she had received a lot of attention from people she didn't know. She showed Jackie a café, and us going downstairs and her lying on the gaps on bits of wood, which would seem to be decking. Now, this did baffle us a bit, as we had no recollection of going anywhere like this with Angel. But, the really amazing part is... a few months later, we went on a family weekend to Centre Parcs. Whilst there, we took Angel to a café which we had to walk down steps to and straightaway, she went and lay down on its decking! To top that, we had so many comments from people saying how lovely she was! Could she actually have known this was going to happen in advance? If so, all I can say is that animals are even more special than anybody could ever have thought. There are so many more incredible things about this world that we can't even begin to understand but Jackie has given us an insight into it and we can't thank her enough.

Angel showed Jackie an image of a photo of Bonzo to the right side of the bed (which she insisted was on the right side of the bed, correct) and of me saying goodnight to him. Oh wow! When we lost him, I had two photo cushions done so that we had one each of him.

We worried that as we were still grieving over Bonzo, that Angel may feel second best and we didn't ever want her to feel that way. She replied, 'Don't worry about that, I could have been a morose soul, but you got a happy dog'. She acknowledged that Bonzo was our first dog, and there is such a thing as first love, but she doesn't feel second best at all. She then went on to say 'I'm very precious! I'm also very understanding of your love for Bonzo!' This really touched us as we thought was a sweet and thoughtful dog Angel is, and that has made us love her even more. All this time we had been worrying about this, but it hadn't bothered her at all. How lucky are we to have yet another special dog in our lives.

When we asked Jackie about Angel being scared of fireworks, Angel told Jackie to tell us to turn the music up loud, and say to her 'It's nothing to do with you, and it can't hurt you' and that she could always wear ear muffs! We started laughing, and she said "Only joking!" However, we did go on to repeatedly say to Angel that it was nothing to do with her when the fireworks started and it did seem to help calm her down a little.

Angel finished off the reading telling Jackie, "I'm a very happy dog!" and that you can take a photo of me from different sides and it would look like you have got two dogs! We couldn't believe it when she volunteered this, as these are exactly the words we had previously said to Mark's mum when she had been visiting. As Angel is mainly white, if you took a photo of her from the right you would see a white dog, but she has a black patch over her left side of her face, so that if you were to take a photo from the other side she would look like a completely different dog. She was literally telling Jackie what we had been saying about her!

This was yet again another lovely reading with Jackie. It is truly lovely to communicate with a living animal also, as we had only previously had a spirit reading. It was so comforting, and reassuring, to know our beautiful little girl was so happy living with us and that she knew she was loved, and in no way second best just because we were still grieving.

Thank you once again Jackie for this very special and comforting reading.

*****

Susan and their dog Archie

In February 2010 my sister's dog Toby sadly passed away. He was 16-years-old. In the following May, she adopted a beautiful male Bichon, named 'Bitza', from the Dogs Trust.

My sister was told that 'Bitza' was about three-years-old. He had been brought there with a female dog and their three puppies. His white fur was so matted, that the trust had had to shave him bare. Sadly, before my sister's adoption of him, he had already been adopted once previously, only to be returned two weeks later.

She decided to rename her new adoption, 'Archie'. A new name, for a new life. My sister hadn't had Archie very long before she became very ill. We (myself and my husband) looked after him each time she had a hospital appointment or stay. (One time, it was for six weeks.)

By the time my sister passed away in December 2012, we had grown to love Archie very much, and so, he came to live with us. We weren't planning to get a dog, having previously owned another that had passed away some years ago. However, what love and joy Archie brought into our lives. He was such a happy, loving boy, and he helped me to get over losing my sister.

Archie was small in stature, but his character was larger than life. He had not had toys before, but soon had many, which he would throw and shake, growling at them as he did. He wasn't used to being brushed, so I made a game of it. I would chase him round the room with his brush and his tail would be wagging with delight. When Archie needed his fur trimmed, we had the groomer come to our home – I distracted him with treats fed to him, in order to keep him in one place!

He would throw his favourite dog biscuits at me, and then he and I would throw them back and forth. Backwards and forwards it would go, until he decided to eat it. Everything was fun to Archie, and for us. Sometimes he would sit in the armchair, head held high in the air and bark, just out of sheer joy.

Archie could not be left on his own, so, where we went, he went too. He enjoyed caravan holidays at the coast, and weekends away. Even simple outings such as our daily walks in the park, visiting the garden centre where he would investigate every shelf, even climbing onto them for a closer look! Pet stores were a favourite on his list too. When we were out, and he saw a large dog, or a cat, (or even better in his own mind a fox!), Archie would pull like stink as he wanted to chase it. He would be barking away, in hot pursuit with us hanging onto his lead for dear life!

People were attracted to Archie wherever we went, especially children. He made people smile. There was something very special about our Archie. Everyone he met loved him – we used to say he was a local celebrity, as he was so well known and admired by many people.

He would get very excited when our son visited which was often. Make no mistake though, when it was bedtime for Archie (which he seemed to instinctively know as being the same time every night), he would sit and stare at our son to tell him it was time to bid his goodnights and leave, then off Archie would go. Archie made the rules, and we happily obliged. Our dear dog was very affectionate spending a lot of time having cuddles on my lap, and at night, he shared our bed.

Unfortunately, he'd had quite a few health issues: having two operations when grass seeds found their way into his ear, resulting in a perforated ear drum – an operation to remove a cyst from his back – a torn cruciate ligament – and on-going allergies that affected his skin. In October 2017, it was discovered Archie had cancer of the spleen, so had his spleen removed to save him and with the hope that it had not spread anywhere else. Whatever life threw at him, he always bounced back with a smile on his face. His attitude to life was utterly inspirational.

Early in 2018 he was diagnosed with a problem with his liver and a few months later, also his kidneys. He was on medication and a suitable home cooked diet. In his last few months of his life, he enjoyed being hand fed which consisted of Archie climbing up, and sitting, on my husband's lap whilst he was fed. He seemed to be doing quite well; even two days before he passed away, the vet felt there was a chance his health would pick up again. Such was the battler that our lad was. Sadly, he quickly deteriorated, and on October 11th, 2018 we had to have him put to sleep.

We wanted Archie to end his life at home. However, because of how he was suffering, it became urgent for him to be at rest, so we had to take him to the vets. We took his own bed with us and were joined by our son, to be there with myself and my husband. It was a very peaceful passing.

Archie's left a huge hole in our lives – we constantly missed the joy he created and revelled in, and on November 20th, we undertook a reading with Jackie, via Skype.

First Jackie described his personality: She said he was a sweet, happy dog, who loved life and affection. He was an inspirational dog who had overcome difficulties in his life. Even when he was older, he had vitality and when he went out, he was interested in everything, sniffing about and investigating. That he was a joy giver and that children gravitated to him. In life, he was a cheeky, happy dog (before his health deteriorated), and that – he still is now.

She continued, that when he came to us, he was rather quiet, but that with us he blossomed and that he was given to me, to help me get over another loss. This was touching as he was my sister's rescue boy and he really did help me through her loss.

Archie said his life with us was full of fun, love and attention. We poured love into him and did whatever we could for him. He was very much a part of the family and that we were the best Mum and Dad. This struck such a chord with me, because every day I would tell him how he was the 'best boy'. He said he only had the best of food, 'no rubbish for me' he quipped, and that he had lovely days out with us. He said that we should still go to the park that he so enjoyed walking around, where there is a boulder – that this should remind us of him, as 'it's not going anywhere'. This made us laugh, as the boulders are huge! So most certainly not going anywhere and loved that in his thoughts, they are there as also a memorial for him. He also mentioned to Jackie, how we took him out in the snow last winter, and instructed her to pass on to us, that when we see dogs paw prints in the snow anywhere, we should think of him.Archie continued on to tell us that we should remember him how he was before any illness, because that's how he is now. He has a little girl called Bethany with him and is playing with a dog called Mitzy. Cheekily, he added, 'There are cats here too' and that he chases them but would never hurt one. Jackie laughed and pointed out that in spirit there is no physical, so no pain, so nobody can get hurt, and so a fun and innocent game for him.

He said to Jackie, before we knew him, he wasn't cared for properly and wasn't groomed. He needed re-homing. This made him so grateful for all the extra care we gave him. Archie told her that my husband would say over and over to him that he was a 'super dog'. We knew straight away what Archie meant – from the time when Archie had torn his cruciate, my husband always carried him up and down the stairs in the house whilst jokily saying, 'Super dogggg, super dog' all the way up, and on the way down too.

Archie said his 'back legs were inflexible' as he got older. Again, this was spot on and Jackie commented that it was an interesting turn of phrase. Eventually he was unable to jump up onto the armchair and sofa. We had put bolster cushions on the floor to act as steps for him, then he was able to get up once again. He continued chatting to Jackie saying that, he loved cuddles and being up next to us. He said that he was slightly deaf but, he could always hear a knife and fork on a plate come dinner time! He most certainly could!

He was very pleased that his ashes have his name on. Again, this last comment amazed us… as his urn does not have his name actually engraved on it. However, one Christmas I was given a silver bauble with his name on, so I had placed it on the urn. Wow, he could see what I had done and I am sure he will be delighted that my son now has a memorial stone with Archie's name on it too.

Archie said his passing was a blissful goodbye. He explained that it was like closing a book and, that when our time comes, he will still be there so we will open the book once more, and start the next chapter together. Jackie said that this was not a description she had heard before, and what a clever, and wise, dog he was for describing the process like this.

Archie told Jackie, he is still close to us and now can even go places with us he couldn't before – as he cannot be seen, so anywhere dogs are not allowed, he would be! What a lovely and happy thought.

Our reading was very emotional, but also Archie made us laugh, as he did every day in life. Jackie described his personality exactly. Also the description of his previous life, and how he had come to live with us was so right. We could absolutely verify everything Archie said about our life together. We were so pleased that he enjoyed his life with us and that he knew how loved he was, and still is. Most importantly, to know that Archie is happy and healthy in Heaven, (and sure to be back with my sister) and that one day, we will be together again. I know our little local celebrity will be so pleased to have his story in Jackie's book.

*****

Charlene and her dog Pele

Pele came into my life in October 2007. Right from the start he was my 'wingman'! He was vibrant, loyal, loving and full of character. I loved him completely from the moment I saw him.

I knew someone that had got a puppy from a place not far from where I lived, so I decided to go and have a look. When I got there, I was led to an outbuilding that had been sectioned off into pens, with dogs of various breeds. I was drawn towards a very lively bunch of black and tan puppies. I distinctly remember how they made it practically impossible not to notice them. As I got closer, the puppies came bounding over, apart from one. He looked like he had separated himself from the others, he was alone and facing the back wall of the pen. Even though I couldn't see his face, I instinctively knew that he was definitely coming home with me.

Just as I was about to tell the breeder that I had chosen my puppy, Pele turned his head and made direct eye contact with me. The connection between us was so strong, I instantly loved him completely, and with my whole heart. This 'knowing' is difficult to explain; I just knew that it was meant to be. I commented to the breeder that Pele was tiny compared to the other puppies, and was told that he was the 'runt' of the litter. It made absolutely no difference to me. This just made me love him even more. From that day onwards he was no longer the 'runt' he was 'Wee Pele'. My beautiful boy!

I had picked Pele up on a Saturday afternoon and had scheduled to take him for a check-up at the Vets on the Monday. Although he was playful, he had been vomiting a lot on both the Saturday, and Sunday evenings. I was convinced that there was something more to it than just the nerves of settling into his new home. On the Monday the vet confirmed that he was small for his age, a little underweight, and that he unfortunately had Kennel Cough. However, after a course of treatment, he was as right as rain! Throughout his entire life I never really had to worry about his health. He had the occasional trip to the Vets but nothing was ever serious. During my reading with Jackie she said that Pele had described himself as a 'Strong Wee Man' and I couldn't have put it better myself; he was so resilient.

Pele loved nothing more than being by my side, it really was his favourite place to be. However, the older Pele got, the more independent he became, and he really did know his own mind! When he had decided that he had had enough of the park, and wanted to go home, he would swiftly take himself back to the car – there was no stopping him. He was off like a shot! I was amazed that he was able to get back to the car safely – when I would get there puffing and panting from chasing after him. He would be so cool like, 'What's all the fuss and, what took you so long?' He made me laugh so much; he was his own man so I could never be angry with him! The park that we went to didn't have a car park with people driving in and out as such. He was not really unsafe to do this, but after a couple of times I decided to always put him back on the lead half way through our walk, to save my nerves, and to avoid any chance of anything bad happening to him.

When I met my husband, I eventually moved in with him and of course Pele came too. My brother-in-law's dog Rocky, who was also a black and tan terrier, decided that he too wanted to move in with us! He simply didn't want to go home... we would insist on taking him back, but as soon as he could escape, he would always be on our doorstep crying to get in. Both Rocky and Pele didn't really like other dogs; they definitely preferred the company of humans, but they loved each other. They developed a very strong bond, and to witness this was amazing! To say they had me wrapped around their little paws, would be a complete understatement. Life was great, and the pair of them would make me laugh on a daily basis. They brought so much joy to my life, but could also be rather mischievous. Rocky was so independent and I truly believe that he, like Pele, thought that he was a human being also. Rocky even taught Pele how to open my front door.

Sadly, Rocky crossed over in January 2016 at the ripe old age of 18. Pele was lost without his buddy, but we still had each other. Slowly, but surely, we got back on track and started to enjoy life again.

The week before Pele crossed over, I took him to the vets. He had unusually become quite fussy over his food, opting only to eat chicken or sliced cooked ham. He also had a little cough but only in the morning when he woke up. The vet carried out a thorough check on him and thought that his liver may be the problem. He gave Pele a course of antibiotics, and prescribed a new vet diet. I tried so hard to stick to this, but Pele had other ideas. He refused point blank to eat the new food. After a few days, I was becoming more and more concerned. I prayed that Pele would just eat. My prayers did not seem to be getting answered, so after speaking to my sister about it, I decided that I was just going to give him what he wanted. However, little did I know that my husband was feeding him exactly what he wanted, without me knowing. At the time, I may have worried about veering from the 'new diet', but looking back I'm so glad that he did this, as Pele definitely seemed to perk up! I think that during that week I forgot that I knew Pele better than anyone, even the vet. In my heart I realised there was something wrong and that he wasn't just being fussy for the fun of it – if I were ever in this situation again, I would definitely follow my instincts.

The night before Pele crossed over will always stay with me... I had decided to watch the Tom Hanks movie 'Castaway' and Pele got up on the sofa beside me and cosied up in my lap and appeared to be watching the film with me. It may seem a very ordinary type of evening, but I remember looking at him and thinking about our bond, and how incredibly happy we made each other. Once again, I was overwhelmed by how much I loved him. He had been by my side through the good times, and the bad, and had never once let me down.

The next night came as an absolute shock to me as Pele had had a good day, and night, and seemed to be on the mend. I had felt relieved as he was happy, and very settled, and that put me at ease. As usual, we both went to bed at the same time. But around 2am, my husband woke me up, as it was clear that something was very wrong. Pele's breathing sounded raspy and he seemed to have a cough. We rushed him to the emergency vets, and after a check-up, some Calpol and an anti-coughing medicine. We were told that he was fine to go home, and they advised us that we should book him in for a chest x-ray in the morning, at his own vets because of the cough. Despite this, the emergency vet was not worried about Pele, and certainly gave no indication that we may be dealing with a life threatening condition. I was just so relieved to be taking my boy home. I thought that he would get the chest x-ray in the morning and maybe some more antibiotics, and then all would be well.

Unfortunately, things didn't go that way as planned. When we got home Pele didn't really settle, and I had a terrible gut feeling that we were on borrowed time. After about 30 minutes he wanted to get off my bed, but couldn't seem to co-ordinate himself to get down. I lifted him down and he went to his own bed for a few minutes. He then got up and walked around to my husband's side of the bed, then headed for the door. Just prior to leaving the room he stopped, turned his head and gazed into my eyes... in this moment I was transported back to the very first time that we had met.

Pele was not walking properly and seemed slightly dazed, so I told my husband that we had to go back to the vets. When I phoned the vets they said that the medication they had given him could have made him woozy, but I knew that it was more serious than that, and told them that we were bringing him back in. This all occurred within an hour of bringing him home! I wrapped Pele in his cosy blanket and carried him to the car, he was limp but still very much conscious. With my husband driving, and Pele on my lap, I remember feeling completely panic stricken. We had only been in the car for a few minutes when everything changed; it all happened so fast.

When we arrived at the vets (about ten minutes after leaving home) immediately they asked if they could try to resuscitate him. After several failed attempts, they felt that they had no option but to stop. My world had just collapsed, my heart shattered into a million tiny pieces, and I was utterly numb, confused and devastated. The pain I felt was simply immense, I was heartbroken.

After a few days I started looking online and found Jackie's website, I downloaded her book, and then emailed to ask for a reading. At this point I was still devastated and not really in control of my emotions. Jackie wisely advised me to wait a few weeks in order for me to be emotionally ready. I took her advice, and I am so glad that I did.

Before speaking to Jackie I was so nervous; I was worried that I would get upset and cry my eyes out, but it was quite the opposite – I immediately felt at ease! Jackie actually made me laugh, and I definitely was not expecting that. She told me that Pele had described himself as a beautiful dog, trustworthy, very friendly, soft and soppy, just like a best friend. I couldn't have agreed more! Jackie also accurately explained the events of the night of Pele's passing. However, through Pele, she was also able to give me more information; it was like the missing pieces of a puzzle were being put back together again. I was overwhelmed that Jackie could have known what happened in such detail. She said that Pele had told her that his passing was very quick and that he was not in any pain. He confirmed that he had had an internal obstruction that had been growing and that there were no choices to be made – so it had all been taken out of our hands. He also said that he was glad that he didn't have a long suffering because I couldn't have coped with that. He explained that I would have gone into an absolute panic, which I would have done. Pele also confirmed that if humans could choose this way of passing on, they would.

Pele's passing was very traumatic for me, but through Jackie I felt a sense of peace. Having Pele's input on the situation was invaluable and helped to put my mind at ease. To hear that he did not suffer was so important to me. Jackie also talked about a memorial I had for Pele and he liked that. She went on to describe a bracelet that I had got from a friend as a Christmas present. I had received the bracelet after Pele had crossed over, so I was pretty blown away! This provided further proof that she was in fact connecting to him and he was still watching over me.

Pele also told Jackie that he liked it when I would tell him where I was going. If I ever forgot to say to him, he would soon let me know. He would come charging down the hallway and barking at me, and as soon as I'd say, 'Mummy is going to work', he would just stop.

Jackie told me so many wonderful things and really gave me proof that Pele's spirit is very much alive and well. Another example of this is that a few days following Pele's transition, I had a conversation with my cousin about putting a large photo of Pele up, but not sure where it was going to go. He suggested that my en-suite bathroom would be the perfect place as Pele loved to lay in front of the bath when I was in it. I laughed and said, 'No way' and I thought that it was a terrible idea. However, during my reading with Pele, he brought it up and declared that he thought it was actually a great idea, and if I was worried about 'steam', I could always get it laminated! As mentioned, initially I wasn't keen on the suggestion but since Pele likes the idea, I will definitely get round to doing it. Even now he still has me wrapped around his paws. Bless him.

Pele told both Jackie and I that he had an extra dimension to his life now. He said that there was an 'etheric life' and that he was a 'conduit'. After Jackie did a quick check on Google to clarify, she found; A 'conduit' is a messenger, a channel that can be used to pass messages through. Mind blowing! He said that he can do even more good for me where he is now than he ever could have done whilst he was here. Pele gave me very clear instructions of what he thought would be good for me. I have followed his direction and will continue to explore and expand my own awareness of the 'spirit world'. Jackie told me that she was amazed at how strong the connection was with Pele, and how powerful he was at validating what he was feeling. This made me feel incredibly proud of him.

As we were nearing the end of our chat I asked if there was anything that Pele wanted me to know and here is what he said,

'There is nothing in life to really fear, because the answer is always there.'

Immediately Jackie said, 'Oh wait a minute, he wants to change it so it rhymes!" This made me laugh again. The final version of that amazing and beautifully touching comment is as follows.

'There is nothing in life to really fear, because the answer is always here.'

It was an absolute honour and privilege to be able to speak to Jackie. She really has helped me in dealing with, my grief. I now fully trust and believe that death is not the end. My journey with Pele continues!

My beautiful boy I love you now, always and forever. I am as proud to be yours, as you were to be mine.

*****

Jill and her dog Mas

To say that Mas (pronounced Maz) was my world, would be an understatement. I often told her she was my Angel without wings. She was a present for me on one of the hardest days of my life ever. In fact, I have to admit, I was really thinking a puppy is not what I want at this point in my life. However, as she was to tell Jackie 15 years later; she was the best thing to ever happen to me, and how very right she was.

I roll back to those years gone by and explain why my heart was in pieces. My husband knew he was going to pass over very soon and arranged with my children to go and get a Yorkshire Terrier pup for me. Not just any old pup, complete with description... a totally fawn face complete with lovely pointy ears! My children set about this finding task and found her available to collect and fitting the description. They travelled to get her and brought her home. She knew my husband Charlie for eight hours, yes only eight hours as he then passed away. As you can imagine, I was bereft, but she was my last gift from him. Although a challenging part of my life, I looked after this young puppy the best I could as I muddled through this terribly sad time.

She grew by the day and with that, her personality did too. She really was so very special, I was about to share my life with the most wonderful, and funny little girl, ever! She truly was my saviour and my shadow, which is why once again my heart is broken. I took her everywhere I could with me. Although at home, she would bark quite a bit for my attention and showing me what she thought was the next thing to do to amuse me! However, when she was out, she would sit on my lap so quietly (she was not really a lap dog) like 'butter wouldn't melt' and people adored her.

She was like forever young and even at over 15-years-old, she was still going strong and enjoying life just the same. At 15 years and 8 months, suddenly one evening she really didn't seem her usual self. Her breathing had altered and although she did not seem to be in pain, or that anything major was going on, I sat up all night with her, giving her all the love and tender care my heart could.

I got her into the vets first thing but my usual vet was away on holiday, so I was greeted by a lady vet called Kiay. She was so gentle with Mas and me, she even gave me a hug. She said she would do all that she could to help her, as it seemed very likely that Mas had fluid on her lungs. Kiay said to leave her with them at the surgery, they would check her lungs and do some blood tests to see what was going on. I felt relieved and thought all would be well, after all, only the day before she still ran to the gate to bark at the postman.

Later that day, Kiay phoned and asked me to come in. I thought it would be to simply pick her up with some treatment but this was actually to be her last trip home... Kiay gently explained to me that not only did Mas have fluid on her lungs, but also her kidneys were failing due to the fact that she had a tumour. I think my heart actually momentarily stopped as I heard those words. I got my breath back and asked how long had she got? Kiay replied that actually, she needed to be put to sleep, today. I was now in shock but Kiay explained that although she had seemed fine, there was much going on inside her. As difficult as this was to listen to, Kiay said it is fortunate that the tumour had not burst as they so often do at such an advanced stage. I tried to take this on board and she even said that sometimes when this happens people have to see their dogs pass blood or throw it up etc. It would be so unfair to let this happen to such a beautiful little dog you love so very much, and her you. This way, at least she would have a peaceful passing and that is how you will remember it.

I drew a deep breath and said that I wanted it done at home. Kiay agreed and that she would come to my house later that day. I put my darling Mas in the car and set off home in floods of tears and my mind in a complete spin. How could I have not known she was ill? How could I have not known all this was going wrong inside of her? How am I ever going to cope without her? How am I going to get hold of my children and tell them what little time we had left? The questions were endless and going round and round in my mind. When we got home, I knew I had a few hours left with her so decided to make the most of loving and comforting her and saying all that I could think of, which is what I did.

Kiay arrived and comforted me and then gave Mas a sedative. Kiay sat me down and putting Mas comfortably in my arms. Mas was calm and I kissed her and kissed her and talked to her as she got sleepy and then had her last ever injection. My heart was pounding in my chest with the pain and loss but at least it was peaceful, and she got to pass away gently in my arms. The next few hours and days were a blur, but I had a lot of support and got her cremated so I could have her back with me as best as possible.

I do believe in spiritual things and I had been reading Jackie's animal communication column in Chat it's Fate magazine – it's the first thing I read! So, after a few months, I wrote into them to see if Jackie would contact Mas for me and thank goodness I did.

I booked an appointment that got cancelled as Jackie had flu and had lost her voice. We re-booked then I got flu, so third time lucky, we actually spoke.

Jackie explained that she would give me what she got and Mas opened the conversation saying that she was a delightful soul and had never seemed old. My goodness, that was just so her and even to her last day, she seemed young. Mas said that she loved people and was a real people pleaser. Jackie laughed and said that she thought that Mas was maybe in charge and seemed to 'direct' me. Oh so true! She was bossy and I let her. Mas heard me and pointed out that she was polite with it!

Mas's next line made us both laugh. She, in her own words, informed us that she, 'kept her weight, didn't suffer from underweight'. That was her version of admitting that she was a little overweight, but put beautifully in her own way. Knowing Mas as I did, I even commented that it was 'So Mas'!

Jackie talked to Mas about why she had gone to Heaven and gently told me that there seems to be a few things that had gone wrong, and very quickly. She mentioned her kidneys and breathing and Mas said that although young on the outside, she had aged on the inside. Too much was wrong so irreparable. I told Jackie that the vet had found the same and sadly a tumour too.

Jackie explained that if we look upon their (and our) bodies like cars; once of older years with use and having wear and tear, frequently when one bit starts to go wrong, so does the next and the next. However, incredibly animals often do not show anything until the very last day of their lives. I asked the same question that had haunted my mind, as to why I had not noticed anything. Jackie was quick to explain that the reason was because Mas had not shown you any signs of illness at all. Jackie went on to tell me that through her work, she has been shown many dog's many times that had seemed absolutely fine, showing no indication of any immediate problems and certainly no signs of a tumour. They had been for a walk, ate their breakfast etc and then suddenly collapsed because a tumour inside them starts to bleed, or bursts.

Sadly, this is such a shock for the owners and can mean sometimes their animal will throw up, or pass blood, and all very distressing. My brain recalled the same conversation that Kiay had said about blood etc. Suddenly, the weight had been lifted off my shoulders and I now knew that it was the right thing to let her go when I did. Now I am thinking more logically – I could not see inside her to see what was going on, nobody could. I can now grieve without guilt.

'Bedtime was bedtime' Mas stated. So true; she danced about and danced about until I gave in and we went to bed.

Jackie said she knew I had said to her, 'Do you know how much I love you?' It was as if she was trying to mimic my accent. I said it so often and checked with her if she really did know how much. Mas re-assured me and said how much she truly loved me and being with me. Jackie told me that Mas referred to herself as your Angel. I was overwhelmed with this as I often used to say to her, 'You are my Angel without wings.'

Jackie was talking about Mas watching out of the window. I was trying to hold my emotions together and explained that she did that a lot of the time as it is full length glass. I said I could not bear to wipe her nose prints off the glass, so they are still there. Jackie suggested that I get a lipstick (quickly checking with me that I did have some, and I do!) and to choose an area to draw a circle around, so it will never be wiped away. This way you can at least safely clean most of the window. She then said, what about a heart shape? The choice was mine and I said it had to be a heart. I have done that and now feel that memory is safe on the glass surrounded by a heart of love.

'Back home safe and sound,' Mas said. Jackie said she thought this meant she was in an urn. I answered that she is. We talked about a special framed photo of her. I told Jackie I take it to bed with me at night and place it on my husband's pillow at the side of me. Jackie gently asked me if my husband had passed over. I said, 'Yes' to which Jackie responded, 'He's been away a while.' I agreed and Jackie asked if his name began with 'M'? I said no, as he was called Charlie. She said, that she was sure Mas was showing her a big M, but not to worry, no problem. I then went on to tell Jackie about him getting her for me just before he died. I said that is why she is called Mas after him, so she was always to be Mas. Jackie then said, 'I thought his name was Charlie?' 'Yes,' I replied 'it was but his nickname was Mas.' (This was due to his surname.) Jackie laughed and said, 'Err, do you remember the big 'M' I was shown?' It then clicked and I said, 'Yes.' It is funny how your brain can go blank sometimes. It made us both laugh, which was lovely.

Jackie said to think of me now gifting Mas to Charlie and I said that is very much like what the vet wrote in her poem. 'The vet wrote you a poem?' Jackie asked seeming rather surprised. 'Oh yes, can I read it to you?' 'Of course.' ' Here it is…'

A Poem For A Patient

Your faithful companion and friend

Arranged with love at Charlie's end

Her life filled with love, right from the start,

Her mum so caring, never wanting to part.

Fifteen years is a grand old age

But bodies start to fail at that stage,

We had to make a very hard choice,

As little Mas had no voice

To let her go into a forever sleep

No more illness just us to weep.

Little Mas was tired and it was her time to leave'

Though it doesn't make it easy

For her mum that's left to grieve.

But remember Jill, she's free from pain

She'll have been met by Charlie calling her name.

She knows you loved her with all your heart,

She knows it hurts you to be apart.

No more illness no more struggles,

She's with Charlie receiving snuggles

And someday when the time does come,

She will be waiting to greet her mum.

Kiay – August 2019

Well, Jackie was stunned and admitted to being opened-mouthed throughout. Kiay's words and summary of Mas, me, and my life, and loss, were incredible. What is also amazing is that I had only met Kiay a couple of times and she was, in essence, simply my vet for Mas. I was so very touched, amazed and totally overwhelmed and overjoyed, all in one. Jackie said that Kiay is one in a million, such a wonderful, compassionate and thoughtful vet, and is probably very spiritual to have written such incredible words.

Losing Mas is such a deep deep heartache and I know in time I will learn to live with it and am thankful every day for having had her. Through this grief journey I have been so kindly cared for by friends and family and found a vet that touched me more than words can write. Fortunately by reading Jackie's column, I learnt that animal communication (living and spirit) existed and thanks to Jackie, my heart and mind are at peace and my healing journey can begin. Until then, and our meeting up again in Heaven, I know I am so blessed to have had Mas and Jackie to connect with her for me. I know I still have a hard journey ahead but Mas my darling Angel, now with wings, fly free and give love to Charlie for me too.

*****

Postscript

I say a huge thank you to my friends: Shirley, Tara, Kathy and Karen, for being my post-checkers after my editing efforts. Your help is invaluable. Also to Moyra for her help and support too. Moyra had her fabulous children's book, *Amelie Trott and the Earth Watchers,* published this year. It is about saving the planet and animals (that talk!) are at the core of it. I am so proud of her.

Talking of publishing, you may be surprised to realise, that I do not actually have the usual 'traditional' type publisher (not for the want of trying) and do all my books myself. It is a huge amount of work (and an incredible amount of emails!) which I do not mind, and I am proud of, however, I would love for them to be promoted further afield and to spread the word about animal communication, which publishing houses do for the authors who are taken on.

Without an agent, it is hard to get even listened to, let alone someone read your manuscript. Although, I have to say, years ago when I was doing my *Celebrity Pet Talking* book, one was interested my work. However, he did suggest that I should spice up / embellish my stories more! I would not do that as my stories are the actual truth and not full of extra 'fillers' to increase the page count. I know that my books stir emotions and help people in many ways, just as they are. Did they do that for you?

So, nine books later, and more in the pipeline, if by any chance, you have connections to an agent / publisher etc. and you think that they may be able to help me get my books into the bigger marketplace (and maybe translated across the world etc. as I most certainly cannot do that for myself) please drop me a line. It may sound odd me even writing this, however, I believe that I am being guided to put this out to the universe this way, so let's see what happens.

Thank you for choosing and reading my book and if you like what I do and want to read more, here are the other books that I have written too.

They are all available on Amazon in paperback and digital. If you don't mind me asking... but if you can

spare a minute to write a review about this book (or other ones of mine that you have read) I would be most grateful. It is the public's opinion that helps others make their choice of reading material. So, if you feel this book would be informative, enjoyable or even enlightening to someone else, a few words would help guide them.

If I have worked for you and you think people would like to read your story, then feel free to email me on info@animalpsychic.co.uk and we can go from there. Please don't worry if you have not written a story before, I hadn't until my first book! I can give you a bit of guidance and, as long as you write the gist of it, I can do the rest. Bless you all and may you and your animals stay well and safe and do enjoy talking to them knowing that they do understand what you say!

If you want to be kept informed of what I am getting up to, TV appearances, what my next book is etc. I do send out the occasional newsletter. If you go on to my website and scroll down to the bottom of the first page, you will see a picture of my cat and you can sign up from there. I promise, your email address is totally protected, and never shared.

Jackie Weaver
'The Animal Psychic'
www.animalpsychic.co.uk

Printed in Great Britain
by Amazon